The First Year

Of Hell

A Compendium of How Democratic Ideals
Fared Against
Trump Administration Threats in 2017

Sharon L. Cohen

Cover Art Work: Seth Mathurin

ISBN:10:1986741192
ISBN-13-9781986741194

TABLE OF CONTENTS

"Thank you!" to the print and online media for their expert coverage of the Trump Administration from which this information is compiled.

AUTHOR'S NOTE

When I heard that Donald Trump was running for President of the United States, I immediately said, "He's going to win!"

My family and friends disagreed: "You always think the worst! There is no way that he will win." Time went by. The Republican contenders dropped out one by one, the media thoroughly covered "Trump this," and "Trump that," and emails and WikiLeaks defeated Hillary Clinton.

Despite my initial belief that Trump would win, I still hoped that I was wrong. Unfortunately, I joined millions of people who were devastated by the results. In the morning, we spent hours on the phone and at coffee shops commiserating, not so much about Clinton's loss but what this meant for democracy. How much would the country change under the Trump Administration? Would all Obama advances vanish? How strong was the U.S. Constitution against a major force of change in the White House and the Republican majority?

I kept track of the daily news and was soon spending a lot of time recording all the people, places and events that were impacting "life as we knew it." Soon, it even became difficult for the media to keep up, as several "news-breaking" stories were reported at the same time.

Of course, this compendium would be completely different if written from a Republican and/or pro-Trump perspective. Given my political and social views, the information contained specifically details how the White House, Cabinet and Congress are altering the Democratic gains over the past eight years--or more. Sadly, it also demonstrates how the country is moving backward in time well beyond these eight years. Racial equality; freedom of religion, speech and press; LGBTQ rights; women's personal rights; climate control; clean environment; free trade; refugee resettlement; immigration; election integrity; and, most of all, government ethics are all struggling or even beginning to fail under the Trump Administration.

I provide specific information on the cabinet members' background and actions; Executive Orders written or eliminated by the White House; Trump supporters and detractors; foreign affairs; Trump fitness for the Presidential role and the White House-Russian connections over the past two years. Although this guide primarily deals with Trump, you should also be concerned about how the Republican Congress is/is not acting, the future of the U.S. Supreme Court, and the involvement and direction of Vice President Pence. The latter has been very quiet and removed from the President, which sets off a lot of alarms about what he plans on doing if/when Trump leaves his office. For example, Pence has stated "Abortion will end in our time." Pence called Moral Majority Co-Founder Paul Weyrich a "friend and mentor." According to Jane Mayer of *The New Yorker,* "Weyrich condemned homosexuality, feminism, abortion, and government-imposed racial integration, and he partnered with some controversial figures, including Laszlo Pasztor, a former member of a pro-Nazi party in Hungary."

This guide can be troubling, but we must also take note of the positive events of the past year. Large numbers of adults--younger and older--are now politically involved, many more women--Democratic and Republican--are running for office in 2018, and there is a resurgence of national interest from centrists, the left and right. That is Democracy--the goal of caring, committed citizens to consider the best interests of all Americans. I hope this book provides helpful information that encourages everyone to strive for what is right and fair for all.

CHAPTER ONE: ONLY DOWN FROM HERE

Inauguration. Despite detailed aerial photographs and metrics, Trump claimed he had the "largest crowds ever." at an inauguration. He said 1.5 million people attended his. "That was the largest audience to witness an inauguration, period. Both in person and around the globe." However, the estimate was closer to 250,000 people. One million attended Barack Obama's 2013 inauguration, down from 1.8 million in 2009. In 2005, 400,000 went to George W. Bush's inaugural event after 300,000 did the same in 2001. For Bill Clinton, the numbers were 800,000 in 1993 and 250,000 in 1997.

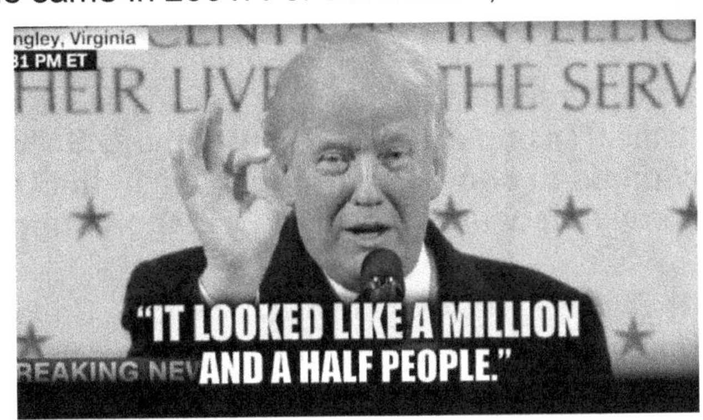

At one point in the inaugural proceedings, Trump turned to talk to his wife Melania, who stood smiling behind him. When he once again faced the crowd, her smile immediately turned into a scowl. No one knew the reason for her change in emotion. Did he say something that disturbed her or was it concern about what was to come?

"Alternate Facts." Counselor to the President Kellyanne Conway explained how Press Secretary Sean Spicer used "alternative facts" when saying Trump had the largest inauguration crowds ever. And, thus, a whole new phrase was introduced, and the Trump reign became a nonstop series of alternate facts.

Popular Vote. Winning the election was not enough for the President. He needed to win the popular vote, as well. Thus, Trump complained of voting fraud. Following the election, the administration reported that over 3 million noncitizens voted in the election, and this would be proved. No proof has been given since. A study by the Brennan Center for Justice at the New York University School of Law found only 30 incidences of noncitizen voting out of 23.5 million votes cast in select jurisdictions having the highest populations of noncitizens. That means only 0.0001% of votes were cast by noncitizens

Executive Orders. In his first year, Trump signed more executive orders (EOs) than any other president in the past 50 years. This was ironic, considering he greatly criticized Obama's use of such orders: "Obama goes around signing executive orders. He can't even get along with the Democrats. He goes around signing all these executive orders. It's a basic disaster. You can't do it."

Some "Basic Disasters" Covered in Trump's EOs:

Travel Ban. Trump wanted to ban people who were coming to the U.S. primarily from Muslim countries. The President's ban was quickly challenged through the legal system and had to be changed. The six countries approved in the final ban were Chad, Iran, Libya, Somalia, Syria and Yemen. North Korea and Venezuela were later added. The U.S. Supreme Court made the travel ban fully operational In December 2017.

In January, 2018, nearly one year after Trump issued his initial ban on travel from Muslim countries, the U.S. Supreme Court agreed to resolve a challenge to a third, more refined version. In *Trump v Hawaii,* the Court will hear arguments on whether Trump's travel ban, Proclamation No. 9645, also known as Executive Order 3 (EO-3), violates the Establishment Clause. This issue involves allegations that by applying the ban against Muslim countries based on religion the Trump Administration may have showed favoritism to religions.

Transgender Students' Bathroom Use. The Trump Administration rescinded protections for transgender students in public schools. The move by the U.S. Justice and Education Departments reversed Obama, who said a federal law known as Title IX protected the right of transgender students to use restrooms and locker rooms that match their gender identities. **(Trump also weeted that the U.S. "will not accept or allow ... Transgender individuals to serve in any capacity" in the U.S. military." This request was later withdrawn because of lack of Pentagon support.)**

Refugee Resettlement. The U.S. State Department told refugee agencies it was sharply reducing the number of offices across the country authorized to resettle people in 2018. The decision is leading to the closure of numerous resettlement offices around the country, potentially leaving some refugees without access to services that could integrate them into American life. Overall, the number of refugees allowed to resettle was cut from Obama's ceiling of 110,000 to 45,000, the lowest since the modern program was established in 1980.

Sanctuary Cities. Trump tried to financially punish sanctuary cities, which have shielded undocumented immigrants from deportation. A San Francisco judge blocked the order, since Congress--not the President--has control over federal spending. The order also violated the Fifth and Tenth Amendments of the Constitution. In November 2017, U.S. District Court Judge William Orrick issued a permanent injunction blocking Trump's EO.

Election Integrity. This EO ignored Russian involvement in the U.S. election and instead focused on voter fraud, despite all evidence that such fraud has been extremely rare. Trump established the Presidential Advisory Commission on Election Integrity to "study the registration and voting processes used in federal elections, including 'vulnerabilities' that allow for fraudulent voting." The commission requested voting records from each state. Most states did not send this information for fear of how it was going to be used. The commission was sued by the Electronic Privacy Information Center and the American Civil Liberties Union. It was shut down in January 2018 due to "endless legal battles."

Free Speech and Religious Liberty. This EO targeted the Johnson Amendment prohibits religious groups from endorsing political figures and concerns the mandate for employers to subsidize birth control coverage. Changing the amendment altogether would require Congressional action. This EO is on par with court cases, such as the one for Hobby

Lobby, which ruled that corporations with religious owners cannot be required to pay for insurance coverage of contraception. If Attorney General Jeff Sessions uses this EO to his advantage, no religious belief would be too minor to exempt an organization from complying with federal law. Corporations and organizations receiving taxpayer dollars would be able to determine which federal regulations they follow. If Sessions' interpretation is challenged and affirmed by the U.S. Supreme Court, the EO can change the law for a lifetime.

Border Wall. Trump signed an EO ordering the Secretary of Homeland Security to "take all appropriate steps to immediately plan, design, and construct a physical wall along the southern border." He also took steps to enlarge U.S. resources for capturing and detaining undocumented immigrants, such as increasing border patrol agents and detention centers. The EO nixed the "catch and release" policy, which allowed undocumented immigrants to be set free on humanitarian grounds rather than be detained.

Crime Reduction. Three EOs directed the U.S. Attorney General to establish a Crime Reduction and Public Safety Task Force; target transnational drug cartels by telling federal agencies to "increase intelligence" sharing; and use current federal laws to prosecute anyone who commits violence against law enforcement. These orders contradicted the historic decrease in crime and ignored the impact on communities of color that have been disproportionately singled out by law enforcement.

America-First Offshore Energy Strategy. Trump signed an EO that directed the Bureau of Ocean Energy Management to develop a five-year plan for oil and gas exploration in offshore waters and to look at several regulations for these activities. Another order established the new position of Counselor to the Secretary for Energy Policy, who will oversee the Interior Department's energy portfolio across nine of its ten bureaus.

Interior Secretary Ryan Zinke said these orders were aimed at unleashing America's offshore energy potential and growing economy: "Following through on the leadership established by President Trump, today's orders will help cement our nation's position as a global energy leader and foster energy independence and security for the benefit of the American people, while ensuring that this development is safe and environmentally responsible. We will conduct a thorough review of the Outer Continental Shelf for oil and gas exploration and listen to state and local stakeholders. We also will conduct a thorough review of regulations that were created with good intentions but have had harmful impacts on America's energy security."

The Trump administration had thus promoted the most sweeping offshore drilling plan in American history, with plans for extensive drilling in the Arctic, Atlantic and Pacific as well as parts of the previous off-limit areas of the Gulf of Mexico. Experts said this proposal called for a five-year drilling plan for 2019 to 2022 that consisted of over 90% of the entire outer continental shelf, some areas where drilling had never occurred or experienced such exploration in decades. In short, Trump wants to allow drilling for gas and oil along the whole U.S. coast. It is believed that this area holds 90 billion barrels of oil and 319 trillion cubic feet of natural gas, or 80% more than what has been available over time. Zinke said this order would make the U.S. the strongest energy superpower the world has ever known. A joint letter from 64 environmental groups responded that this would cause "severe and unacceptable harm" to U.S. publicly owned oceans, coastal economies and marine life.

Trump Executive Actions in 2017

Signature Date	Subject
January 20	Minimizing the Economic Burden of the Patient Protection and Affordable Care Act Pending Repeal
January. 24	Expediting Environmental Reviews and Approvals for High Priority Infrastructure Projects
January. 25	Border Security and Immigration Enforcement Improvements
January 27	Protecting the Nation from Foreign Terrorist Entry into the United States
January 28	Regarding Ethics Commitments by Executive Appointees
January 30	Reducing Regulation and Controlling Regulatory Costs
February. 3	Core Principles for Regulating the United States Financial System
February. 9	Enforcing Federal Law with Respect to Transnational Criminal Organizations and Preventing International Trafficking
February 24	Enforcing the Regulatory Reform Agenda
Feb. 28	The White House Initiative to Promote Excellence and Innovation at Historically Black Colleges and Universities
Mar. 6	Protecting The Nation From Foreign Terrorist Entry Into The United States (revision of 13769)
Mar. 13	Comprehensive Plan for Reorganizing the Executive Branch

Mar. 27	Revocation of Federal Contracting Executive Orders
Mar. 28	Promoting Energy Independence and Economic Growth
Mar. 29	Establishing the President's Commission on Combating Drug Addiction and the Opioid Crisis
Mar. 31	Establishing Enhanced Collection and Enforcement of Antidumping and Countervailing Duties and Violations of Trade and Customs Laws
Mar. 31	Regarding the Omnibus Report on Significant Trade Deficits.
Mar. 31	Providing an Order of Succession Within the Department of Justice
Apr. 18	Buy American and Hire American
Apr. 21	Identifying and Reducing Tax Regulatory Burdens
Apr. 25	Promoting Agriculture and Rural Prosperity in America
Apr. 26	Enforcing Statutory Prohibitions on Federal Control of Education
Apr. 26	Review of Designations Under the Antiquities Act
Apr. 27	Improving Accountability and Whistleblower Protection at the Department of Veterans Affairs
Apr. 28	Establishment of the American Technology Council
Apr. 28	Implementing an America-First Offshore Energy Strategy
Apr. 29	Addressing Trade Agreement Violations and Abuses
Apr. 29	Establishment of the Office of Trade and Manufacturing Policy

May 4	Promoting Free Speech and Religious Liberty
May 11	Establishment of the Presidential Advisory Commission on Election Integrity
May 11	Strengthening the Cybersecurity of Federal Networks and Critical Infrastructure
June 15	Expanding Apprenticeships in America
June 21	Amendment of Executive Order 13597
June 30	Revival of the National Space Council
July 11	Amendment of Executive Order 13761
July 19	Establishing a Presidential Advisory
July 21	Assessing and Strengthening the Manufacturing and Defense Industrial Base and Supply Chain Resiliency of the United States
Aug. 15	Establishing Discipline and Accountability in the Environmental Review and Permitting Process for Infrastructure
Aug. 25	Imposing Additional Sanctions With Respect to the Situation in Venezuela
Aug. 28	Restoring State, Tribal, and Local Law Enforcement's Access to Life-Saving Equipment and Resources
Sept. 20	Imposing Additional Sanctions with Respect to North Korea
Sept. 29	Continuance of Certain Federal Advisory Committees
Sept. 29	Revocations of Executive Order Creating Labor-Management Forums
Oct. 12	Promoting Healthcare Choice and Competition Across the United States
Oct. 20	Amending Executive Order 13223
Oct. 24	Resuming the United States Refugee Admissions Program with Enhanced Vetting

	Capabilities
Dec. 8	Revising the Seal for the National Credit Union Administration
Dec. 20	A Federal Strategy To Ensure Secure and Reliable Supplies of Critical Minerals
Dec. 20	Blocking the Property of Persons Involved in Serious Human Rights Abuse or Corruption
Dec. 22	Adjustments of Certain Rates of Pay

Republican Legislation

Tax Bill. The final bill heavily favored tax cuts for corporations and business owners. There were some perks for individuals, but they were small and finite, unlike those for companies. The tax bill is jam-packed with provisions and delayed tax increases to help its compliance with budget rules. Yet it also hides its potential real cost; if policymakers down the road do not let these provisions take effect, the bill's cost would be about $2.2 trillion over the first decade (2018 to 2027) or nearly 50% more than the Joint Committee on Taxation's official cost estimate of $1.5 trillion. Economist Larry Kudlow said the bill will pay for itself, with a much lower deficit and economic growth of 3 to 4%.

Business Impact

Cut corporate income tax rate permanently to 21% from 35%, as of Jan. 1, 2018.

Created a 20% deduction for the first $315,000 of qualified business income for joint filers of pass-through businesses such as partnerships and sole proprietorships. For income above that threshold, it phased in limits, producing an effective marginal tax rate of no more than 29.6%.

Repealed the 20% corporate alternative minimum tax, established to ensure profitable corporations pay at least some tax.

Exempted U.S. corporations from U.S. taxes on most future foreign profits, ending the present worldwide system of taxing profits of all U.S.-based corporations, no matter where earned. It thus aligned the U.S. tax code with most other industrialized nations

Set a one-time mandatory tax of 8% on illiquid assets and 15.5% on cash and cash equivalents for about $2.6 trillion in U.S. business profits now held overseas..

Prevented companies from shifting profits out of the U.S. to lower tax jurisdictions abroad. Set an alternative minimum tax on payments between U.S. corporations and foreign affiliates and limits on shifting corporate income through transfers of intangible property, including patents. These measures represented a dramatic overhaul of the U.S. tax system for multinationals.

Allowed businesses to immediately write off, or expense, the full value of investments in new plant and equipment for five years and then gradually eliminate 100% expensing over five years beginning in year six. Also made changes to allow for more expensing by small businesses.

Capped business deductions for debt interest payments at 30% of taxable income, regardless of deductions for depreciation, amortization or depletion.

Preserved tax credits for producing electricity from wind, biomass, geothermal, solar, municipal waste and hydropower.

Left the "carried interest" loophole for private equity fund managers and some hedge fund managers.

Individual Impact

Maintained present seven tax brackets, but temporarily changed most income levels and rates for each.

For married couples filing jointly, effective Jan. 1, 2018 and ending in 2026, income tax would be:

10% up to $19,050, versus 10% up to $18,650 under existing law;
12% on $19,051 to $77,400, versus 15% on $18,651 to $75,900;
22% on $77,401 to $165,000, versus 25% on $75,901 to $153,100;
24% on $165,001 to $315,000, versus 28% on $153,101 to $233,350;
32% on $315,001 to $400,000, versus 33% on $233,351 to $416,700;
35% on $400,001 to $600,000, versus 35% on $416,701 to $470,700
37% above $600,000, versus 39.6% above $470,700.

For single individuals, effective Jan. 1, 2018 and ending in 2026, income tax would be:

10% up to $9,525, versus 10% up to $9,325 under existing law;
12% from $9,526 to $38,700, versus 15% on $9,326 to $37,950;
22% on $38,701 to $82,500, versus 25% on $37,951 to $91,900;
24% on $82,501 to $157,500, versus 28% on $91,901 to $191,650;
32% on $157,501 to $200,000, versus 33% on $191,651 to $416,700;
35% on $200,001 to $500,000, versus 35% on $416,701 to $418,400;
37% above $500,000, versus 39.6% above $418,400.

These brackets would expire after 2025.

In a change expected to end itemizing of deductions for millions of Americans, the bill for eight years beginning on Jan. 1, 2018, increased the standard deduction - a fixed amount that can be subtracted from adjusted gross income to lower taxable income - to $12,000 from $6,350 for individuals, and to $24,000 from $12,700 for married couples.

It doubled the child tax credit to $2,000 per dependent child under age 17, with a refundable portion of $1,400. The refundable portion allowed families to lower their tax bills to zero and to receive a refund for the remaining value.

It temporarily eliminated the $4,050 individual personal exemption. Under previous law, taxpayers earning below certain income caps could subtract this fixed dollar amount from their adjusted gross incomes to lower taxable incomes. Generally, one exemption has been allowed per individual, spouse and child or other dependent. This took effect Jan. 1, 2018, **but then the personal exemption would return in 2026.**

The bill left the alternative minimum tax in place but temporarily changed it by raising exemptions and phase-outs, meaning fewer people will have to pay the tax and those who still do will take a smaller bang..

It raised the exemption for estate and gift taxes $5 to $10 million per person and indexed the new exemption level for inflation after 2011. Fewer Americans will need to pay the estate tax, but it does stay on the books.

For residences bought from Jan. 1, 2018, through Dec. 31, 2025, the bill capped the deduction for mortgage interest at $750,000 in home loan value. After Dec. 31, 2025, the cap reverts to $1 million in loan value. It suspends the deduction for interest on home equity loans from Jan. 1, 2018 until 2026.

It temporarily expanded the deductibility of out-of-pocket medical expenses through 2019.

Favors to Get the Needed Vote Numbers:

To all the Republicans who wanted to repeal (and replace) the ACA, the bill repealed federal fine imposed on Americans under Obamacare for not obtaining health insurance coverage, a change expected to undermine the ACA. Senator. Lisa Murkowski received her allowance for oil drilling in Alaska's Arctic National Wildlife Refuge.

The Total of Trump Laws

NPR analyzed and categorized the 96 laws signed by Trump from Congress in 2017. Over.37 modified or extended existing law; 16 repealed rules and regulations through the Congressional Review Act; 12 commemorated people and organizations, for example renaming federal buildings; and 7 provided temporary government funding or one-time disaster relief funds.

Types Of Laws Signed By Trump In 2017

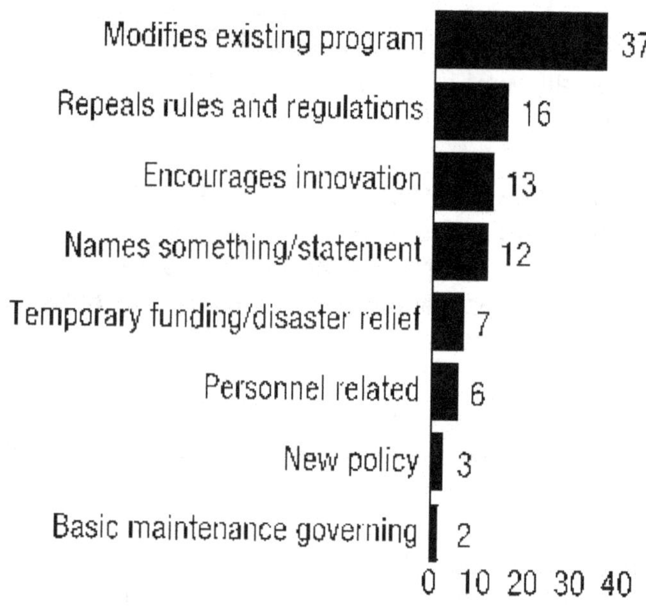

Maintained

- <u>HR 244</u> Consolidated Appropriations Act, 2017
- <u>HR 2810</u> National Defense Authorization Act for Fiscal Year 2018

Implemented New Policy

- <u>S 1094</u> Department of Veterans Affairs Accountability and Whistleblower Protection Act of 2017
- <u>HR 3364</u> Countering America's Adversaries Through Sanctions Act
- <u>HR 1</u> An Act to provide for reconciliation pursuant to titles II and V of the concurrent resolution on the budget for fiscal year 2018 (tax bill)

Temporarily Funded Government, Provided One-Time Disaster Relief

- <u>HJRes 99</u> Making further continuing appropriations for fiscal year 2017, and for other purposes
- <u>HR 601</u> Continuing Appropriations Act, 2018 and Supplemental Appropriations for Disaster Relief Requirements Act, 2017
- <u>HR 3732</u> Emergency Aid to American Survivors of Hurricanes Irma and Jose Overseas Act
- <u>HR 3823</u> Disaster Tax Relief and Airport and Airway Extension Act of 2017
- <u>HR 2266</u> Additional Supplemental Appropriations for Disaster Relief Requirements Act, 2017
- <u>HJRes 123</u> Making further continuing appropriations for fiscal year 2018, and for other purposes
- <u>HR 1370</u> Continuing Appropriations Act, Department of Defense Missile Defeat and Defense Enhancements Appropriations Act, CHIP and Public Health Funding Extension Act, 2018

Repealed Rules and Regulations (way to reverse earlier regulations)

- <u>HJRes 67</u> Disapproving the rule submitted by the Department of Labor relating to savings arrangements established by qualified State political subdivisions for non-governmental employees
- <u>HJRes 43</u> Providing for congressional disapproval under chapter 8 of title 5, United States Code, of the final rule submitted by Secretary of Health and Human Services

relating to compliance with title X requirements by project recipients in selecting subrecipients

- HJRes 69 Providing for congressional disapproval under chapter 8 of title 5, United States Code, of the final rule of the Department of the Interior relating to "Non-Subsistence Take of Wildlife, and Public Participation and Closure Procedures, on National Wildlife Refuges in Alaska"
- HJRes 83 Disapproving the rule submitted by the Department of Labor relating to "Clarification of Employer's Continuing Obligation to Make and Maintain an Accurate Record of Each Recordable Injury and Illness"
- SJRes 34 A joint resolution providing for congressional disapproval under chapter 8 of title 5, United States Code, of the rule submitted by the Federal Communications Commission relating to "Protecting the Privacy of Customers of Broadband and Other Telecommunications Services"
- HJRes 4 Disapproving the rule submitted by the Department of Labor relating to drug testing of unemployment compensation applicants
- HJRes 57 Providing for congressional disapproval under chapter 8 of title 5, United States Code, of the rule submitted by the Department of Education relating to accountability and State plans under the Elementary and Secondary Education Act of 1965
- HJRes 58 Providing for congressional disapproval under chapter 8 of title 5, United States Code, of the rule submitted by the Department of Education relating to teacher preparation issues
- HJRes 37 Disapproving the rule submitted by the Department of Defense, the General Services Administration, and the National Aeronautics and Space Administration relating to the Federal Acquisition Regulation
- HJRes 44 Disapproving the rule submitted by the Department of the Interior relating to Bureau of Land Management regulations that establish the procedures used to prepare, revise, or amend land use plans pursuant to the Federal Land Policy and Management Act of 1976
- HJRes 4 Providing for congressional disapproval under chapter 8 of title 5, United States Code, of the rule submitted by the Social Security Administration relating to Implementation of the NICS Improvement Amendments Act of 2007
- HJRes 38 Disapproving the rule submitted by the Department of the Interior known as the Stream Protection Rule
- HJRes 41 Providing for congressional disapproval under chapter 8 of title 5, United States Code, of a rule submitted by the Securities and Exchange Commission relating to "Disclosure of Payments by Resource Extraction Issuers"
- S 496 A bill to repeal the rule issued by the Federal Highway Administration and the Federal Transit Administration entitled "Metropolitan Planning Organization Coordination and Planning Area Reform"
- HJRes 66 Disapproving the rule submitted by the Department of Labor relating to savings arrangements established by States for non-governmental employees
- HJRes 111 Providing for congressional disapproval under chapter 8 of title 5, United States Code, of the rule submitted by Bureau of Consumer Financial Protection relating to "Arbitration Agreements"

Encouraged an Agency or President To Try New Approach

- <u>HR 321</u> Inspiring the Next Space Pioneers, Innovators, Researchers, and Explorers (INSPIRE) Women Act
- <u>HR 255</u> Promoting Women in Entrepreneurship Act
- <u>HR 534</u> U.S. Wants to Compete for a World Expo Act
- <u>HR 274</u> Modernizing Government Travel Act
- <u>HR 366</u> DHS SAVE Act
- <u>S 327</u> Fair Access to Investment Research Act of 2017
- <u>S 810</u> A bill to facilitate construction of a bridge on certain property in Christian County, Missouri, and for other purposes
- <u>S 1141</u> Women, Peace, and Security Act of 2017
- <u>HR 1117</u> To require the Administrator of the Federal Emergency Management Agency to submit a report regarding certain plans regarding assistance to applicants and grantees during the response to an emergency or disaster
- <u>S 190</u> Power And Security Systems (PASS) Act
- <u>S 920</u> National Clinical Care Commission Act
- <u>HR 194</u> Federal Agency Mail Management Act of 2017
- <u>HR 1545</u> VA Prescription Data Accountability Act 2017

Reauthorized or Modified Existing Programs/law

- HR 353 Weather Research and Forecasting Innovation Act of 2017
- S 442 National Aeronautics and Space Administration Transition Authorization Act of 2017
- S 419: Public Safety Officers' Benefits Improvement Act of 2017
- S 583 American Law Enforcement Heroes Act of 2017
- HR 72 GAO Access and Oversight Act of 2017
- HR 657 Follow the Rules Act
- S 1083 A bill to amend section 1214 of title 5, United States Code, to provide for stays during a period that the Merit Systems Protection Board lacks a quorum
- HR 3218 Harry W. Colmery Veterans Educational Assistance Act of 2017
- HR 1238 Securing our Agriculture and Food Act
- HR 3298 Wounded Officers Recovery Act of 2017
- HR 374 To remove the sunset provision of section 203 of Public Law 105-384, and for other purposes
- HR 510 Rapid DNA Act of 2017
- HR 2430 FDA Reauthorization Act of 2017
- HR 339 Northern Mariana Islands Economic Expansion Act
- HJRes 76 Granting the consent and approval of Congress for the Commonwealth of Virginia, the State of Maryland, and the District of Columbia to enter into a compact relating to the establishment of the Washington Metrorail Safety Commission
- HR 2288 Veterans Appeals Improvement and Modernization Act of 2017
- S 1866 Hurricanes Harvey, Irma, and Maria Education Relief Act of 2017
- S 652 Early Hearing Detection and Intervention Act of 2017
- S 544 A bill to amend the Veterans Access, Choice, and Accountability Act of 2014 to modify the termination date for the Veterans Choice Program, and for other purposes
- S 114 VA Choice and Quality Employment Act of 2017

- <u>HR 3819</u> Department of Veterans Affairs Expiring Authorities Act of 2017
- <u>S 585</u> Dr. Chris Kirkpatrick Whistleblower Protection Act of 2017
- <u>HR 1329</u> Veterans' Compensation Cost-of-Living Adjustment Act of 2017
- <u>HR 1616</u> Strengthening State and Local Cyber Crime Fighting Act of 2017
- <u>S 504</u> Asia-Pacific Economic Cooperation Business Travel Cards Act of 2017
- <u>S 782</u> PROTECT Our Children Act of 2017
- <u>HR 304</u> Protecting Patient Access to Emergency Medications Act of 2017
- <u>HR 3031</u> TSP Modernization Act of 2017
- <u>HR 3243</u> FITARA Enhancement Act of 201
- <u>HR 3949</u> VALOR Act
- <u>HR 4374</u> To amend the Federal Food, Drug, and Cosmetic Act to authorize additional emergency uses for medical products to reduce deaths and severity of injuries caused by agents of war, and for other purposes
- <u>HR 228</u> Indian Employment, Training and Related Services Consolidation Act of 2017
- <u>S 371</u> Department of State Authorities Act, Fiscal Year 2017, Improvements Act
- <u>S 1266</u> Enhancing Veteran Care Act
- <u>HR 624</u> Social Security Number Fraud Prevention Act of 2017
- <u>S 178</u> Elder Abuse Prevention and Prosecution Act
- <u>HR 1679</u> FEMA Accountability, Modernization and Transparency Act of 2017

Named Something/Sites Memorial Encouraged Flag-Flying/ Made Statement

- <u>SJRes 1</u> A joint resolution approving the location of a memorial to commemorate and honor the members of the Armed Forces who served on active duty in support of Operation Desert Storm or Operation Desert Shield
- <u>HR 1362</u> To name the Department of Veterans Affairs community-based outpatient clinic in Pago Pago, American Samoa, the Faleomavaega Eni Fa'aua'a Hunkin VA Clinic
- <u>HR 609</u> To designate the Department of Veterans Affairs health care center in Center Township, Butler County, Pennsylvania, as the "Abie Abraham VA Clinic"
- <u>S 305</u> Vietnam War Veterans Recognition Act of 2017
- <u>HR 375</u> To designate the Federal building and United States courthouse located at 719 Church Street in Nashville, Tennessee, as the "Fred D. Thompson Federal Building and United States Courthouse"
- <u>HR 873</u> Global War on Terrorism War Memorial Act
- <u>HR 2210</u> To designate the community living center of the Department of Veterans Affairs in Butler Township, Butler County, Pennsylvania, as the "Sergeant Joseph George Kusick VA Community Living Center"
- <u>SJRes 49</u> A joint resolution condemning the violence and domestic terrorist attack that took place during events between August 11 and August 12, 2017, in Charlottesville, Virginia, recognizing the first responders who lost their lives while monitoring the events, offering deepest condolences to the families and friends of those individuals who were killed and deepest sympathies and support to those individuals who were injured by the violence, expressing support for the Charlottesville community, rejecting White nationalists, White supremacists, the Ku Klux Klan, neo-Nazis, and other hate groups, and urging the President and the President's Cabinet to use all available resources to address the threats posed by those groups
- <u>S 1616</u> Bob Dole Congressional Gold Medal Act
- <u>HR 2519</u> The American Legion 100th Anniversary Commemorative Coin Act

- <u>HR 2989</u> Frederick Douglass Bicentennial Commission Act
- <u>S 1617</u> Javier Vega, Jr. Memorial Act of 2017

<u>Related to Personnel</u>

- <u>SJRes 30</u> A joint resolution providing for the reappointment of Steve Case as a citizen regent of the Board of Regents of the Smithsonian Institution
- <u>SJRes 36</u> A joint resolution providing for the appointment of Roger W. Ferguson as a citizen regent of the Board of Regents of the Smithsonian Institution
- <u>SJRes 35</u> A joint resolution providing for the appointment of Michael Govan as a citizen regent of the Board of Regents of the Smithsonian Institution
- <u>HR 1228</u> To provide for the appointment of members of the Board of Directors of the Office of Compliance to replace members whose terms expire during 2017, and for other purposes
- <u>S 84</u> A bill to provide for an exception to a limitation against appointment of persons as Secretary of Defense within seven years of relief from active duty as a regular commissioned officer of the Armed Forces
- <u>HR 3110</u> Financial Stability Oversight Council Insurance Member Continuity

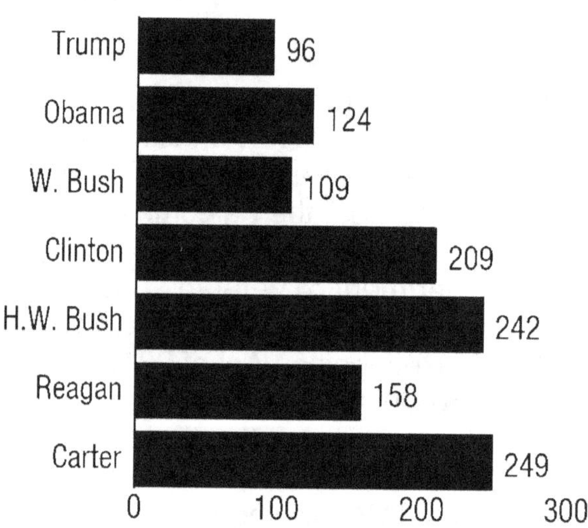

<u>Deferred Action for Childhood Arrivals (DACA).</u> This compendium could not be published without covering DACA, which continues in limbo. Obama's policy shielded 700,000+ undocumented immigrants who came to the U.S. as children. They received a renewable two-year period of deferred action from deportation and eligibility for a work permit. Trump cancelled DACA as a concession to his base but recognized that the "Dreamers'" plight is very important to Americans. He thus passed the decision to Congress with a March 2018 deadline. Congress has not come to any agreement, and the courts' decisions are altering the circumstances. Two district court judges ordered the White House to keep accepting DACA renewal applications until courts consider the way Trump abruptly ended the program. The Administration has sked the Supreme Court to intervene, but it said it is staying out of decision for now.

CHAPTER TWO: WHITE MALE WHITE HOUSE

When asked about the makeup of Trump's cabinet and White House staff, Press Secretary Sarah Huckabee Sanders dodged the answer saying, "We have a really diverse team across the board at the White House." For his cabinet, Trump chose just one African-American with Ben Carson and one Asian-American with Elaine Chao. U.N. Ambassador Nikki Haley is Indian-American and Labor Secretary Alexander Acosta is Hispanic. There are only five women.

President Trump's Original 2017 Cabinet

Administrator of the Environmental Protection Agency Scott Pruitt

Administrator of the Small Business Administration Linda E. McMahon

Attorney General Jeff Sessions

Director of National Intelligence Daniel Coats

Director of the Central Intelligence Agency Mike Pompeo

Director of the Office of Management and Budget Mick Mulvaney

Representative of the United States to the United Nations Nikki R. Haley

Secretary of Agriculture Sonny Perdue

Secretary of Commerce Wilbur L. Ross, Jr.

Secretary of Defense James Mattis

Secretary of Education Elisabeth Prince DeVos

Secretary of Energy James Richard Perry

Secretary of Health and Human Services Alex Azar

Secretary of Homeland Security Kirstjen Nielsen

Secretary of Housing and Urban Development Benjamin S. Carson, Sr.

Secretary of the Interior Ryan Zinke

Secretary of Labor Alexander Acosta

Secretary of State Rex W. Tillerson

Secretary of Transportation Elaine L. Chao

Secretary of the Treasury Steven T. Mnuchin

Secretary of Veterans Affairs David J. Shulkin

U.S. Trade Representative Robert Lighthizer

Vice President Michael R. Pence

White House Chief of Staff John F. Kelly

FBI Director Christopher Wray

The Swamp Became Many Times Swampier

Trump pledged to clean out the swamp, but it has become much fuller and murkier. Although a few of the cabinet members were supported   by both Democrats and Republicans, most of them are wealthy business executives, retired military men, conservative activists and longstanding Trump supporters who do not have the best interests of Americans at heart..

<u>Attorney General Sessions.</u> In 2017, except for run-ins with Trump about his recusal, Sessions seemed to be having a field day. In addition to getting away with lie after lie when testifying to Congress, Sessions proved all his detractors right through his anti-immigrant, racist and inhumane actions.

Sessions followed Trump's lead by trying to destroy Obama's legacy. In February, he fully endorsed private prisons for federal inmates. He ignored previous reports that criticized privatization and noted in a letter that the Obama administration's policy "impaired the bureau's ability to meet the future needs of the federal correctional system. Therefore, I direct the bureau to return to its previous approach."

Sessions supported the Trump Administration on immigration policies. In April, he advised nine sanctuary cities that they had to demonstrate proof of compliance. In July, he added that these cities would not be eligible for millions of dollars in funds for policing. Chicago and

Philadelphia then sued Sessions and the Justice Department, and in November, a federal judge permanently blocked Trump's EO on sanctuary cities.

The AG also ordered a review of Obama reform agreements between the Justice Department and local police departments. He said, "It is not the responsibility of the federal government to manage non-federal law enforcement agencies." Sessions said these agreements demoralized policing agencies, but civil rights proponents argued they helped produce necessary reforms.

In defiance of Obama's policies, Sessions directed federal prosecutors to "pursue the most serious, readily provable offense" with the lengthiest sentences in all criminal cases. This rescinded a 2013 memo by Attorney General Eric Holder, who told prosecutors to avoid mandatory minimum sentences for certain nonviolent, low-level drug offenders.

In 2015, a coalition of 64 Asian-American groups filed a complaint against Harvard University, which was dismissed by the Department of Education due to another similar case pending. The Justice Department reopened this investigation into use of race in admissions policies. This action led to concerns that the administration would target affirmative action policies at other U.S. universities and colleges.

Sessions came after the American poor, too. He rescinded a 2016 Justice Department letter advising local courts against hitting indigent defendants with stiff fines and fees. This letter stipulated that changes were "needed to guarantee equal justice under law to everyone, regardless of their financial circumstances." Sessions said he was repealing this and 25 similar documents, since they were "unnecessary, inconsistent with existing law or otherwise improper." The move provoked a firestorm, leading critics to decry it as a "criminalization of poverty" and a "return to debtors' prisons."

Rounding out his year of successful actions, Sessions overturned Obama's memos that promoted non-interference with marijuana friendly state laws. This potentially paved the way for the government to take legal action on the pot industry. Eight states and D.C. allow personal pot consumption. This policy permits each state's U.S. attorney to determine whether or not to enforce the federal marijuana law, even when the substance is legal in their state. Critics state that Sessions is using federal law enforcement to further his personal view that all marijuana use is wrong. This is what drove the prohibition of alcoholic beverages in the U.S. from 1920 to1933, which proved unsustainable as has the total federal ban on marijuana.

Of all cabinet members, it is Sessions who has made the greatest impact by working to completely revamp U.S. immigration on his own terms. He told the states that federal law "is the supreme law of the land," and his policies supersede all regardless of Sanctuary Cities. He cancelled the legal decision that asylum seekers must have their day in court and separated immigrant parents and children and placed them in different shelters. Presently, the government faces 670,000 immigration cases, as the number of noncriminal immigrant arrests skyrockets.

Secretary of State Rex Tillerson. This new cabinet member joined Exxon-Mobil in 1975 and became CEO in 2006. During his tenure, he developed close ties to Russian President Vladimir Putin; Exxon also had numerous business contracts with Russia. In 2013,

Putin awarded Tillerson the Order of Freedom, the highest honor for a foreign citizen. Although Tillerson was not prepared for his cabinet member position, he has not always sided with Trump on foreign affairs, such as his views on North Korea. This brought him close to the firing line a few times during the year.

The New York Times accused Tillerson of being unfit for diplomatic leadership and determined to dismantle his own department, which has been central to American national security since the time of Thomas Jefferson. The department has been undermined by budget cuts, a failure to fill top jobs and low morale. *Newsweek* added that Tillerson has been throwing out high-ranking women, black and Latino diplomats. Tillerson has stopped most hiring in his department and plans to oust some 2,000 career diplomats by the end of 2018, reported *The New York Times*. At least 30 nations do not have U.S. ambassadors.**(The week this book was published, Trump boosted Tillerson out and chose CIA's Mike Pompeo to take his place.)**

At the end of 2017, *Newsweek* reported that Senators John McCain and Jeanne Shaheen and House Democrats on the Foreign Affairs Committee denounced Tillerson's efforts that are "undermining America internally as complex global crises are growing externally." For example, the United Arab Emirates has been linked to efforts being made to have Tillerson emoved from his post for his attempts at mediation in the Gulf states' feud with the kingdom of Qatar..

<u>Secretary of the Treasury Steven Mnuchin.</u> The swamp became thicker with this Yale graduate and former Goldman Sachs partner. He founded a hedge fund and transformed a failed mortgage lender into One West Bank, criticized for its foreclosure practices. Mnuchin was national finance chair of Trump's presidential campaign. When submitting papers for his background check, he failed to mention $100 million in real estate assets

When Mnuchin married for the third time, he wanted a government plane to transport the happy couple to Scotland, France and Italy. This would have cost $25,000 an hour. He justified the request by saying he needed a military aircraft for security purposes and confidential communications. Much to his chagrin, his request was denied.

Mnuchin has not always considered the consequences of his actions. He and his new wife celebrated the first printed batch of dollar bills bearing his signature in a publicity stunt of the two of them holding a big dollar bill. The visual, which went viral, received "thumbs down" on and off the Internet.

<u>Secretary of Housing and Urban Development</u>
<u>Ben Carson.</u> A retired neurosurgeon, Carson dropped out of the 2016 race for President and supported Trump. Another Yale graduate, he criticized government assistance programs as excessive and said individual efforts were more effective.

At his confirmation hearing, Carson explained he no longer backed the extreme cuts he had supported when running for President. He called such cuts "cruel and unusual punishment." However, he soon was supporting a proposed $6 billion cut and, in early 2018, favored Trump's increased slash to $8.8 billion. "The proposed budget is focused on moving more people toward self-sufficiency through reforming rental assistance." He later added, "I am confident HUD will deliver on its core programs, assist our most vulnerable populations, and make significant enhancements to our programs where needed." As this book was going to press, Carson had to return a $31,000 dining set he purchased for his office with government funds. His daughter-in-law unfairly received a $485,000 consulting contract.

<u>Secretary of Education Betsy DeVos.</u> She had the dubious honor of receiving the most negative critiques during the Senate confirmation process. She was opposed by teachers' unions and public-school advocates. A billionaire, Republican fundraiser and Michigan activist, DeVos has strongly supported publicly funded, privately operated charter schools and vouchers. She stated, "Not all schools are working for the students that are assigned to them. I'm hoping we can work together to find common ground... I believe in equality, and I firmly believe in the intrinsic value of each individual, and that every student should have the assurance of a safe and discrimination-free place to become educated."

DeVos explained that parents have the right to personal choices on whatever school they feel is best for their children. Parents should be able to choose among schools as they do with rideshare options, such as Lyft, Uber or a taxi. "Near the Department of Education, there aren't many restaurants. But you know what? Food trucks started lining the streets to provide options. Some are better than others, and some are even local restaurants that have added food trucks to their businesses to better meet customers' needs. Now, if you visit one of those food trucks instead of a restaurant, do you hate restaurants? Or are you trying to put grocery stores out of business? No. You are simply making the right choice for you based on your individual needs at that time. Just as in how you eat, education is not a binary choice. Being for equal access and opportunity — being for choice — is not being against any anything,." she commented. DeVos said her success will be based on how much school choice expands during her tenure.

DeVos said that her department is changing the Obama Administration's promise of completely erasing loans taken out by students defrauded by the Corinthian Colleges chain. Under the new standards, forgiveness is to be tied to students' income as a way of measuring whether they did gain some benefit from their education.

The Education Secretary has also talked about reducing "the federal footprint in education," so that more authority is given to the states. She called Obama regulations "harmful and costly." Such regulations were largely supported by consumer groups, because they protected students and taxpayers. Too often, for-profit schools are guilty of fraudulent practices and leave students deep in debt with little career prospects.

DeVos also showed her true feelings about civil rights. Soon after being nominated, she called historically black colleges and universities (HBCUs) "pioneers of school choice." This, however, ignored the reason why such schools first arose: African-American students were not allowed in white institutions and had no option but to go to schools created especially for them.
DeVos stated, "They (HBCUs) started from the fact that there were too many students in America who did not have equal access to education. They saw that the system wasn't

working, that there was an absence of opportunity, so they took it upon themselves to provide the solution. HBCUs are real pioneers when it comes to school choice. They are living proof that when more options are provided to students, they are afforded greater access and greater quality. Their success has shown that more options help students flourish."

After a backlash from these comments, DeVos erased the "pioneers of school choice" notion. Senator. Claire McCaskill of Missouri called the statement "Totally nuts. DeVos pretending that establishment of historically black colleges was about choice not racism."

Handling criticism has not been easy for DeVos, calling people who do not share her vision for school choice "defenders of the status quo" and "flat-Earthers." In one speech, she told the audience that "The point is to provide quality options that serve students so each of them can grow. Every option should be held accountable, but they should be directly accountable to parents and communities, not to Washington, D.C., bureaucrats. In order to succeed, education must commit to excellence and innovation to better meet the needs of individual students. Defenders of our current system have regularly been resistant to any meaningful change. In resisting, these 'flat-Earthers' have chilled creativity and stopped American kids from competing at the highest levels. Our current framework is a closed system that envelopes choices and embraces the future."

DeVos has also been supportive of Trump's proposed budget cuts for education. Trump said he wanted to reduce the federal government's role in schools and universities, proposing a $9 billion cut or 13% of the budget. Yet, he would like to see an increase in school choice. In the administration's budget proposal, millions of dollars would go toward charter-school and voucher programs. Another $1 billion in grant funding would be utilized to encourage states to adopt school-choice policies.

<u>Secretary of Transportation Elaine Chao.</u> She was Secretary of Labor under George W. Bush and Deputy Transportation Secretary under George H.W. Bush. She is married to Senator Mitch McConnell, the Senate's Majority Leader. In confirmation hearings, Chao suggested public-private partnerships could be used to build or replace aging bridges and roads. "Deregulation is the key to the success of the infrastructure plan."

<u>Secretary of Labor Alexander Acosta.</u> He previously served as a member of the National Labor Relations Board and as the U.S. Attorney for the Southern District of Florida. He later served as chairman the board of U.S. Century Bank, which is headquartered in Miami and billed as one of the largest Latino community banks in the country. At Trump's urging, the Labor Department announced at the end of 2017 that it wanted to undo an Obama-era regulation that stopped employers from collecting and redistributing workers' tips if the workers earned the federal minimum wage of $7.25 per hour. Department officials said the new rule would non-wait staff to get a share of tips.

Acosta tried to defend a rule that would allow restaurants to take workers' tips, but New York Democratic Rep. Rosa DeLauro stopped him. During a House Appropriations Committee hearing, DeLauro demanded answers from Acosta about his new ruling. because senior officials at the Labor Department apparently withheld studies indicating that workers could lose billions of dollars and restaurant managers and owners would most likely benefit.

<u>Secretary of Energy Rick Perry.</u> He was former governor of Texas (and "Dancing with the Stars" contestant.) When running as president in 2011, he said the Energy Department was one of three he would eliminate if elected. He has also called climate change a hoax. Perry was severely critical of Trump in the 2016 race for President but later became a supporter. He stated upon his nomination, "My past statements, made over five years ago, about abolishing the Department of Energy do not reflect my current thinking. In fact, after being briefed on so many of the vital functions of the department of energy, I regret recommending its elimination."

The Energy Secretary said he hoped to subsidize disappearing and dirty electricity sources, like nuclear and coal, due to the stability that they provide to the grid. He said his plan would compensate facilities that store fuel on-site, because they provide to the country's economic and national security. The Federal Energy Regulatory Commission (FERC) totally rejected this bailout saying, " Secretary Perry likes to use flash and glitz to cover over imperfections in form. Like the wise judges on "Dancing with the Stars," FERC saw through the act."

America now relies less on coal and nuclear energy than ever before, since the energy market is moving toward renewable sources. Perry's plan would cost taxpayers over $10.5 billion a year. "I think it's really important for people to understand, in general terms, there is no free market in the energy industry," Perry explained.

<u>Small Business Administrator, Linda McMahon.</u> She was CEO of World Wrestling Entertainment (WWE). Developed from a business first established by McMahon and her husband, it is estimated at over $1 billion. WWE events were held at the Trump Plaza in the 1980s, and Trump is a member of the WWE Hall of Fame. McMahon donated $6 million to Trump's campaign in 2016 and spent about $100 million in two unsuccessful campaigns In Connecticut for Senate.

<u>Ryan Zinke, Secretary of the Interior.</u> He was a Navy SEAL for 23 years before entering politics as a Montana Congressman. He was a proponent of U.S. energy independence and has said he doubts climate change exists. In a speech before oil and gas industry executives, Zinke argued that the production and transportation of wind turbines contributes to global warming. He also echoed Trump's long-held argument that wind turbines kill birds. "We probably chop us as many as 750,000 birds a year with wind and the carbon footprint on wind is significant," Zinke said. "I always thought the best place for wind was on the roof of a house."

Zinke also said his agency should be a partner with oil and gas companies that seek to drill on public land and that long regulatory reviews with an uncertain outcome are "un-American."

<u>(Retired) General James Mattis, Secretary of Defense.</u> This general led deployments in Kuwait, Afghanistan and Iraq. Before retiring, he was Chief of U.S. Central Command, in charge of all American forces in the Middle East. Nicknamed "Mad Dog" and "Warrior Monk," he is recognized for his leadership in combat.

<u>Sonny Perdue, Secretary of Agriculture.</u> He switched from the Democratic to Republican Party and was Governor of Georgia from 2003 t0 2011. After earning a doctorate in veterinary medicine, he started a number of farming businesses. He served on Trump's agriculture advisory committee during the election campaign. His cousin, David Perdue, is a

Republican senator from Georgia. According to *Mother Jones,* "Over his career in politics he netted $328,328 in donations from agribusiness interests, including $21,000 from Gold Kist, a large, Georgia-based chicken-processing company that was later taken over by chicken giant Pilgrim's Pride."

Mother Jones has also reported a few other unknown facts about Secretary Perdue. He is nostalgic for the Confederacy. In 2010, he signed a law declaring April to be permanently recognized in the Georgia as "Confederate History and Heritage Month." In 2005, Perdue signed one of the first "strict" voter ID laws in former Confederate states. Anyone not having a a current photo identification card will be denied the vote. Perdue vigorously defended the law through it led to several legal challenges, and it has remained in place.

When governor in 2006, Perdue's beliefs about extensive voter fraud were harbingers of those by President Trump: Undocumented immigrants burden taxpayers by siphoning welfare benefits. He said, "It is simply unacceptable for people to sneak into this country illegally on Thursday, obtain a government-issued ID on Friday, head for the welfare office on Monday and cast a vote on Tuesday." He backed up these uncaring words with an attack on undocumented workers. His efforts were so successful that agriculture companies were having difficulty finding enough workers, and now Perdue is looking for ways to keep some undocumented people in the U.S. to help where needed.

Scott Pruitt, Environmental Protection Agency (EPA) Administrator
Previously, he was the attorney general of Oklahoma. His office sued the EPA 14 times on regulatory issues and also filed suit against Obamacare, Dodd-Frank, and executive actions on immigration.

Pruitt agreed with Trump to cut the EPA budget by over 30% Research budgets have been greatly reduced, and many of the staff members are taking buyouts. In 2017, the agency lost more than 700 employees, including 200 scientists. Yet, the EPA is paying for expensive additions, such as a 24-hour security detail and a soundproof booth for Pruitt.

Pruitt announced that his agency would withdraw from the Clean Power Plan, the rule regulating greenhouse gas emissions. He said the scientists are wrong to believe that manmade emissions are the primary cause of climate change. He also argued that EPA has been overstepped its authority with the Clean Power Plan. "God has blessed us with natural resources. Let's use them to feed the world. Let's use them to power the world. Let's use them to protect the world," he stated.

Under Obama, the Waters of the United States rule was to clarify which bodies of water fall under EPA's jurisdiction. The rule extended the protection of the Clean Water Act to two million miles of streams and 20 million acres of wetlands. The 1972 law covered only "navigable waters" — but not necessarily the streams that flowed into them. Pruitt claimed the administration will introduce a clearer alternative to the rule, but no particulars have been given.

Defying the recommendation of the EPA's scientists, Pruitt also refused to ban a widely used pesticide linked to learning disabilities in children. A newly signed order allows the insecticide chlorpyrifos, which has been used on crops from broccoli to cranberries since the 1960s, to remain on the market for agricultural application. Under the Obama administration, the EPA requested the chemical be permanently banned for food crops due to potential risks to human health.

"We need to provide regulatory certainty to the thousands of American farms while still protecting human health and the environment," Pruitt said in a statement. "By reversing the previous administration's steps to ban one of the most widely used pesticides in the world, we are returning to using sound science in decision-making — rather than predetermined results."

Congress told EPA to periodically consider tightening standards for pollutants like smog-forming ozone and lung-damaging soot due to research about effects on human health. Pruitt said he wanted to meet older air quality rules, like the George W. Bush administration's weaker 2008 ozone standard, before focusing on more recent ones. He has not announced which regions have failed to meet the 2015 national air-quality standard, which has delayed the lengthy process for enforcing those limits.

Secretary of Veteran Affairs David Shulkin. A physician, Shulkin was previously Under Secretary of Health for the Department of Veterans Affairs. Until falling into the same trap as other cabinet members by using government funds for his wife's trip to Europe, Shulkin was considered one of Trump's better choices.

Secretary of Homeland Security (retired) General John Kelly. He led the U.S. Southern Command, overseeing military operations in Central and South America and the Caribbean. He served under General Mattis in the 2003 invasion of Iraq. Then, when the White House needed someone to "babysit" the staff, everyone thought that Kelly should change his role to **Chief of Staff**. Unfortunately, this role has shown his true colors. He has made false statements about U.S. Representative Frederica when responding to comments about Trump's insincere condolences to a military widow. Kelly also said Deferred Action for Childhood Arrivals youth were "too afraid" or "too lazy" to sign up for their status. In addition, he supported senior White House official Rob Porter, accused wife abuser, for an undetermined time.

Secretary of Health and Human Services (HHS) Tom Price. It was not long before Price had to resign, because he flew on private and military planes that cost taxpayers nearly $1 million. In early 2018, confirmation hearings for HHS Secretary were then held for Alex Azar, a former HHS official and pharmaceutical executive. Sixty health organizations wrote a letter that urged senators not to vote for Azar, because his stance on the Affordable Care Act (ACA), Medicaid expansion and prescription drug costs has been incompatible with someone who is a "credible advocate for patients." The complaints were not effective, and Azar was confirmed.

Azar met with Idaho's governor and insurance commissioner about altering Obama's ACA. The result has been a much maligned act by the state. Idaho is ignoring ACA rules, and insurers are free to charge the sick more for coverage, to limit their benefits, and to impose annual payout caps. Other states may follow suit if Trump allows Idaho to make these changes.

Secretary of Commerce Wilbur Ross. He made his billions by purchasing and restructuring failing companies, many in manufacturing. He has known Trump since the 1990s and was a campaign supporter. It did not take Trump too long to sour on his new Commerce Secretary, because Ross had been too slow in suggesting trade restrictions.

United Nations Ambassador Nikki Haley. Previously, Haley was a two-term governor of South Carolina. The daughter of Indian immigrants, she once opposed Trump's anti-immigration policies. In the election, she first supported Marco Rubio, then Ted Cruz and finally Trump. She removed the Confederate flag from the South Carolina statehouse after nine black church members were shot and killed by a white gunman in June 2015. Since assuming her role with the U.N., Haley has followed Trump's lead and alienated much of the world against the U.S.

U.S. Deputy Trade Representative Robert Lighthizer. He was sworn the Deputy Trade Representative under President Reagan. He has been a partner in a law firm that represents U.S. steel companies and others in cases of foreign market saturation and subsidies. Lighthizer was an early supporter of Trump and has agreed with the President's views on trade. He's a harsh critic of China's trade practices and the U.S. response.

Director of the Office of Management and Budget and Acting Director of the Consumer Financial Protection Bureau Mick Mulvaney. Mulvaney served in the South Carolina General Assembly from 2007 to 2011, first in the State House of Representatives and then the State Senate. Earlier, Mulvaney had posed the question, "Do we really need government-funded research at all?" Mulvaney, previously a strong deficit hawk, became a proponent of large federal deficits after his appointment to the Trump Administration. Trump's budget proposal shows he has—for now—given up on balancing the budget over the next decade, Mulvaney said at an early 2018 briefing.

CIA Director Mike Pompeo. He was a member of Kansas' U.S. House of Representatives and of the Tea Party movement. He also served as a Kansas representative on the Republican National Committee and a member of the Italian American Congressional Delegation. In late 2017, Pompeo told the Reagan National Defense Forum audience, "I have seen things the President has put on his Twitter account actually have a real-world impact on our capacity to understand what's going on in other places of the world."

However, Pompeo has not always sided with Trump. Joining with FBI Director Wray and Director of National Intelligence Coats, he testify before the Senate Intelligence Committee that Russia is continuing to target the U.S. voting system.

.

Director of National Intelligence Daniel Coats. An Indiana Republican, Coats was U.S. Senator from 1989 until 1999 and then U.S. ambassador to Germany in the first term of President George W. Bush. He then returned to the Senate from 2010 to 2017. During his confirmation proceedings, Coats stated that Russia "definitely did try to influence the campaign." Yet, according to *The Washington Post*, former U.S. officials said that Trump asked Coats to publicly deny evidence of cooperation between his campaign and Russia. These same sources said that Coats refused to comply.

Early in 2018, Coats came out very strong in front of the Senate Intelligence Committee in regard to the U.S. being "under attack" via cybersecurity. Coats also expressed his concern about the militarization of space, climate change and the national debt. Thus far, Trump is remaining quiet on Coats' straying from the script.

FBI Director Christopher Wray. A graduate of Yale University, Wray was nominated by President George W. Bush to be the Assistant Attorney General in the Justice Department's Criminal Division, serving from 2003 to 2005. Wray's tenure has been rocky, since he has not always agreed with Trump. According to Axios, Wray threatened to resign in January 2018 if Deputy FBI Director Andrew McCabe was forced out.

As the Russian investigation became more threatening, Trump stepped up his war against the FBI and top FBI officials.. Wray dismissed allegations against the FBI's incompetency. The Florida school shooting added to this anti-FBI sentiment, with Florida Governor Scott calling for Wray's resignation. However, according to *FirstPost,* a Trump advisor said the President "has full faith in FBI Director Chris Wray."

Who Is Jared Kushner, Anyway?

After playing a star role in Trump's election campaign, Jared Kushner and his wife and Trump's daughter, Ivanka, moved to Washington, D.C. Trump was insistent that his most trusted family members be nearby. Kushner had no political experience, but he was handed or assumed scores of responsibilities, including improving U.S.-China relations, overseeing a taskforce to improve government efficiency, and leading the White House Office of American Innovation. He also pledged to bring peace to the Middle East.

Throughout 2017, Kushner's name was continually in the headlines, and not just for White House responsibilities. During the campaign, Kushner attended a meeting at Trump Towers where a Kremlin-linked lawyer offered access to damaging material on Hillary Clinton and four meetings with Russian officials. In the transition period, he met with Russian Ambassador Sergey Kislyak to discuss establishing a direct line of secure communication from the White House to the Kremlin. It could have been too allow then National Security Adviser Flynn with a direct line to Russia to discuss Syria policy "and other security issues." Until pushed, Kushner did not disclose information on his involvement with Wikileaks or the setting up of the secure line. After the inauguration, Kushner was involved with the firing of FBI Director James Comey.

During 2017, Kushner 's lack of transparency was very evident. He inadvertently omitted dozens of business holdings on his disclosures. When it became clear that over 125 staff members with major responsibilities did not yet have security clearance at the beginning of 2018, Kushner was again singled out due to his reading of high-security information. It became quite apparent that Kushner was not going to receive clearance, considering he continued to amend his financial disclosures, had added millions of dollars in debt during 2017, and had shady contacts with the Russians.

Kushner and Ivanka were in fact hit with a lawsuit by the U.S. District Court in Washington for making illegal omissions on their public financial disclosure forms. It is asserted that the couple failed to identify the assets owned by 30 investment funds in which they were involved. The complaint contended that they should have declared the value of and income derived from their investment vehicles and, in six different cases, Kushner's report indicated that more detailed information was not being provided because a "pre-existing confidentiality agreement" precluded disclosure.

However, "The Ethics in Government Act" (EIGA) does not allow a reporting individual to refuse to disclose the underlying assets of an investment vehicle on this basis, since such disclosure would violate a pre-existing confidentiality agreement. Kushner's attorney called the suit frivolous and said Kushner updated his financial disclosure information several times.

As 2017 was coming to an end, Kushner and Ivanka were not seen as much in the news. This was particularly true after Flynn, Manafort, Gates and Papadopoulus were indicted. Kushner, however, was continuing to push for clearance. Trump handed over the "yea/nay" decision to Kelly.

And What About Ivanka?

In 2017,Ivanka said she was most involved with issues such as women's entrepreneurism, child tax-credit and the economy. She noted that "she likes to stay out of politics. I instead like to focus on areas where I can add positive value, where I can contribute to the agenda." "Policies around workforce development, around ensuring that barriers are removed from around the working family. Policies that enable that family to survive. Focusing on how we can help our veterans–and how we can really deliver them the care that they so need. Focusing on issues related to the really devastating opioid problem we have in this country."

Although she said that her stepmother, Melania, would handle the ceremonial responsibilities, Ivanka was the one involved in a number of such events. At the beginning of 2017, she accompanied her father to Dover Air Force Base to honor the remains of the U.S. Navy SEAL who was killed during a raid on al Qaeda militants in Yemen. She also met with foreign leaders, such as Israeli Prime Minister Netanyahu and German Chancellor Merkel, and was at the Broadway show "Come from Away" with Canadian Prime Minister Trudeau.

Ivanka, like her husband, only has an interim security clearance, and Democrats have called for her removal from White House business. During the year, Ivanka also received a number of lawsuits against her companies. For example, Italian luxury footwear maker, Aquazzura, accused her of copying the company's copyright design. The parties agreed on a settlement before heading to trial. Several stores have also stopped carrying Ivanka's product lines.

Then There Is Donald, Jr.

Like others in the Trump family, Donald, Jr. has found himself embroiled in the Mueller investigation. He changed his story about the June 2017 meeting at Trump Tower with the Russians several times, in part with the suggestions of his father.

Donald, Jr.'s tweets have often been given "thumbs down" by readers. Right before Halloween 2017, he. posted a tweet of his daughter who looked very unhappy with her orange bucket of candy. He said, "I'm going to take half of Chloe's candy tonight & give it to some kid who sat at home. It's never too early to teach her about socialism." Several times, Donald, Jr. supported his father by calling media "fake news."

At the end of 2017, he started a tweeting battle with Jennifer Lawrence after her negative comments about his father. He also erroneously indicated that FBI Deputy Director McCabe was fired. The White House had insisted the President had nothing to do with McCabe's early retirement. After the Parkland shooting, Donald, Jr. tweeted agreement with a conspiracy theory about the shooting.

And Eric...

Although Eric's name was not heard very often during 2017, he had his share of bad news, particularly about his supposed personal charity. The annual Eric Trump Foundation golf invitational had been held for a decade. This event had always been the same: Golfers, including family friends, celebrities, and sports stars played 18 holes, and raised considerable money.

Eric has directed over $11 million to St. Jude Children's Research Hospital, most through this annual golf event. He has also helped raise another $5 million through events with other organizations. Eric said that his connections were the best part of this deal. Since he could use his family's golf course for free as well as mostly donated costs, nearly all the money contributed could help the children most in need.

However, this has not been the case. Instead, it appeared that the course was not free: The Trump Organization received part of more than $1.2 million. Golf charity experts said the listed expenses defied any reasonable cost justification for a one-day golf tournament. Plus, the Donald J. Trump Foundation used the Eric Trump Foundation to funnel $100,000 in contributions into revenue for the Trump Organization. Further, although donors to the Eric Trump Foundation heard their money was going to help children, over $500,000 was re-donated to other charities, many of them connected to Trump personal interests. The most disturbing aspect is that Eric's foundation did donate considerably to the hospital, but he had to stop fundraising through his organization after the election. Eric changed the name of his foundation to Curetivity and continued to raise money through Trump-owned properties.

And Melania, Too

Who is Melania, anyway? Everything is strange in the Trump Administration, including his wife. From the pained look she gave at the inauguration and her desire to end cyberbullying (despite her husband's ongoing bullying), to her reduced visibility during the year, Melania has not been a typical first wife. Plus, she has had to read stories about her husband's affairs while she was pregnant and after delivering.

Then there was the even stranger rumor that Melania had a stand-in body double. It was just a story started by someone on Twitter, but it soon went viral. People were comparing photographs of Melania at different events, as well as the clothes she was wearing, to prove--or disprove--there was a double. This was actually a conspiracy theory that could be understood!

Lastly, Never Forget Mike Pence

With all the actions taken by Trump and his cabinet members, it is easy to forget VP Pence who has been absent at the right times. Pence has his own personal agenda, which continued throughout the year through his speaking engagements with the religious right. As governor, his public health cuts let to a huge HIV outbreak. In 2013, he cut funding for Planned Parenthood by nearly 50%, closing five clinics that never offered abortions, only STD testing. He believes same-sex marriages will lead to a societal collapse and proudly said this past year, "We'll see Roe vs Wade consigned to the ash heap where it belongs."

CHAPTER THREE: A DESOLATE ENVIRONMENT

The New York Times reported that 60 environmental actions were reversed (29 overturned; 24 with current rollbacks; 9 in limbo). Environmental Protection Agency Secretary Pruitt backed almost one-third of reversals that could have severe impacts. The reversals are:

Flood building standards

Proposed ban on a potentially harmful pesticide

Freeze on new coal leases on public lands

Methane reporting requirement

Anti-dumping rule for coal companies

Decision on Keystone XL pipeline

Decision on Dakota Access pipeline

Third-party settlement funds

Offshore drilling ban in the Atlantic and Arctic

Ban on seismic air gun testing in the Atlantic

Northern Bering Sea climate resilience plan

Royalty regulations for oil, gas and coal

Inclusion of greenhouse gas emissions in environmental reviews

Permit-issuing process for new infrastructure projects

Green Climate Fund contributions

Mining restrictions in Bristol Bay, Alaska

Endangered species listings

Hunting ban on wolves and grizzly bears in Alaska

Protections for whales and sea turtles

Reusable water bottles rule for national parks

Environmental mitigation for federal projects

Calculation for "social cost" of carbon

Planning rule for public lands

Copper filter cake listing as hazardous waste

Mine cleanup rule

Sewage treatment pollution regulations

Ban on use of lead ammunition on federal lands

Restrictions On fishing

Paris Climate Accord.. In 2015, representatives from 196 nations agreed to adopt green energy sources, decrease climate change emissions, and limit the rise of global temperatures, while at the same time cooperate on the impact of climate change. These representatives acknowledged that the threat of climate change is "urgent and potentially irreversible." It can only be addressed through "the widest possible cooperation by all countries" and "deed reductions in global emissions."

At the Paris Climate Accord in 2017, Trump decided to throw his weight around and declared, "We're getting out." The U.S. was withdrawing from the accord but would begin negotiations to enter the Paris Agreement or an "entirely new transaction" that would be more "fair" to the U.S. economy. "As someone who cares deeply about the environment, I cannot in good conscience support [the deal]," Trump said, noting that "the Paris Agreement was blocking the development of clean coal in America."

This decision went against the urgings of the European Union and even the Chinese government, which both stood in commitment to the plan, regardless of what the U.S. decided. Several prominent American companies, such as Microsoft, Apple, Google and Facebook, tried to change Trump's mind. They said the E.U. was not going to work with Trump on another approach. "The European Union will not renegotiate the Paris agreement," and "the 29 articles of the agreement must be implemented and not renegotiated.".

Hydraulic Fracking. At the end of 2017, Trump took another anti-environmental step. Fracking rules were proposed under Obama, but they became mired in lawsuits and were never put into effect. These rules would have applied mostly to western U.S. near federal lands. Companies would have had to disclose the chemicals used in fracking, which pumps pressurized water underground to open hydrocarbon deposits. Trump's administration rescinded these proposals, and industry groups praised the decision. They said the federal rules were to duplicate those by the states, which would have put unnecessary burdens on petroleum developers.

Offshore and Arctic Oil Drilling. Trump overturned the 2015 Obama executive order (EO) to ban oil drilling on parts of the Atlantic Ocean and the Arctic. Air-gun blasting, which is a process used for finding oil on the seafloor, is harmful to whales. There has been no drilling in the U.S. since the 1980s.

America-First Offshore Energy Strategy. Trump signed an EO that directed the Bureau of Ocean Energy Management to develop a five-year plan for oil and gas exploration in offshore waters and to look at several regulations for these activities. Another order established the new position of Counselor to the Secretary for Energy Policy for coordinating the Interior Department's energy portfolio across nine of its ten bureaus.

Interior Secretary Zinke said these orders were aimed at unleashing America's offshore energy potential and growing economy: "Following through on the leadership established by President Trump, today's orders will help cement our nation's position as a global energy leader and foster energy independence and security for the benefit of the American people, while ensuring that this development is safe and environmentally responsible. We will conduct a thorough review of the Outer Continental Shelf for oil and gas exploration and listen to state and local stakeholders. We also will conduct a thorough review of regulations that were created with good intentions but have had harmful impacts on America's energy security."

The Trump administration had thus proposed the most sweeping offshore drilling plan in American history, with plans for extensive drilling in the Arctic, Atlantic and Pacific as well as parts of the previous off-limit areas of the Gulf of Mexico. Experts said this proposal called for a five-year drilling plan for 2019 to 2022 that consisted of over 90% of the entire outer continental shelf, some areas where drilling had never occurred or experienced such exploration in decades. In short, Trump decided to allow drilling for gas and oil along the whole U.S. coast. It is believed that this area holds 90 billion barrels of oil and 319 trillion cubic feet of natural gas, or 80% more than what has been available. Zinke said this order would make the U.S. the strongest energy superpower the world has ever known.

In response, a joint letter from 64 environmental groups said that this would cause "severe and unacceptable harm" to U.S. publicly owned oceans, coastal economies and marine life.

Clean Water Rule.. Trump began fighting Obama's EO on federal oversight of pollution in American waters. He first ordered the EPA to "review and reconsider" earlier restrictions. Then, several months later, he rolled back the protections for more than half of the nation's tributaries.

Greenhouse Gas Emissions.. Trump's "Energy Independence" order began dismantling the Clean Power Act, which has mandated that manufacturing plants reduce carbon emissions. The Trump EO reversed the ban on coal leasing on federal lands and reduced restrictions on methane emissions. Several states automatically filed lawsuits, citing endangerment of public health.

National Monuments. Trump signed an EO that defied Obama's use of the 1906 Antiquities Act to protect federal lands from oil drilling and mining. The administration reduced the size of Bears Ears National Monument by 83% and the Bill Clinton-designated Grand Staircase Escalante National Monument by 50%. The most notable change with this EO is how federal public lands can again be open for mining prospectors.

Many environmental groups and Native American tribes mounted lawsuits against the Trump Administration for the monument rollbacks. They said the Antiquities Act does not permit U.S. Presidents to significantly reduce protections. The White House responded that this claim is unfounded.

(In March 2018, Utah Republican lawmaker Mike Noel proposed Utah House Bill 481 to change the name of 631 miles of the "Utah National Parks Highway" to the "Donald J. Trump Utah National Parks Highway," in appreciation for reducing the size of Bears Ears and Grand Staircase national monuments and opening them up for potential mining and oil-drilling. The bill passed with a vote of 9 to 2. "I think he's done a tremendous amount, and I think with seven more years we can turn this country around," Noel said of Trump's actions.)

CHAPTER FOUR: THE UNPOPULAR VOTE

When considering Trump's win, it is difficult to remember all the people who were against his election--and not only the scores of Republican contenders, Hillary Clinton and Bernie Sanders. **Wikipedia** compiled a very thorough list of notable Republicans and conservatives who announced their opposition to the election of Donald Trump. Some of the Republicans supported Trump after he won, while others continued to oppose him..

Former U.S. Presidents

- **George H. W. Bush,** President of the United States (1989–93); Vice President of the United States (1981–89) (voted for Hillary Clinton)
- **George W. Bush,** President of the United States (2001–09); Governor of Texas (1995-2000)

Former 2016 Republican Presidential Primary Candidates

All candidates signed a pledge to eventually support the party nominee. The following refused to honor it after Trump became the Republican presidential nominee.

- **Jeb Bush,** Governor of Florida (1999–2007)
- **Carly Fiorina,** CEO of Hewlett-Packard (1999–2005); 2010 nominee for U.S. Senator from California (originally endorsed Trump for the general election but called for Mike Pence to take his place as nominee after the Access Hollywood Tape surfaced'
- **Lindsey Graham,** United States Senator from South Carolina (2003–present) (voted for Evan McMullin)
- **John Kasich,** Governor of Ohio (2011–present); U.S. Representative from Ohio (1983–2001) (wrote in John McCain)
- **George Pataki,** Governor of New York (1995–2006)

Former Federal Cabinet-level Officials

- **William Bennett,** Director of the Office of National Drug Control Policy (1989–90); United States Secretary of Education (1985–88)
- **Bill Brock,** United States Secretary of Labor (1985-87); United States Trade Representative (1981-85); U.S. Senator from Tennessee (1971-77); Chairman of the Republican National Committee (1977-81)
- **Michael Chertoff,** United States Secretary of Homeland Security (2005–09); Judge of the United States Court of Appeals for the Third Circuit (2003–05) (endorsed Hillary Clinton)
- **Bill Cohen,** United States Secretary of Defense (1997–2001); United States Senator from Maine (1979–97) (endorsed Hillary Clinton) Robert Gates, United States Secretary of Defense

(2006–11); Director of Central Intelligence (1991–93) Carlos Gutierrez, United States Secretary of Commerce (2005–09) (endorsed Hillary Clinton)

- **Carla Anderson Hills,** United States Secretary of Housing and Urban Development (1975–77), United States Trade Representative (1989–93) (endorsed Hillary Clinton)
- **Ray LaHood,** United States Secretary of Transportation (2009–13), U.S. Representative from Illinois (1995–2009)
- **Greg Mankiw,** Chair of the Council of Economic Advisers (2003–05)
- Mel Martinez, United States Secretary of Housing and Urban Development (2001–03); United States Senator from Florida (2005–09); General Chair of the Republican National Committee (2007)
- **Michael Mukasey,** United States Attorney General (2007–09)
- **John Negroponte,** United States Ambassador to the United Nations (2001–04); Director of National Intelligence (2005–07); United States Deputy Secretary of State (2007–09) (endorsed Hillary Clinton)
- **Henry Paulson,** United States Secretary of the Treasury (2006–09) (endorsed Hillary Clinton)
- **Colin Powell,** United States Secretary of State (2001–05), National Security Advisor (1987–89) (voted for Hillary Clinton)
- **William K. Reilly,** Administrator of the Environmental Protection Agency (1989–92) (endorsed Hillary Clinton)
- **Condoleezza Rice,** United States Secretary of State (2005–09), National Security Advisor (2001–05)
- **Tom Ridge,** United States Secretary of Homeland Security (2003–05); Homeland Security Advisor (2001–03); Governor of Pennsylvania (1995–2001)
- **William Ruckelshaus,** Administrator of the Environmental Protection Agency (1970–73, 1983–85) (endorsed Hillary Clinton)
- **George P. Shultz,** United States Secretary of Labor (1969–70); Director of the Office of Management and Budget (1970–72); United States Secretary of the Treasury (1972–74); United States Secretary of State (1982–89)
- **Louis Wade Sullivan,** United States Secretary of Health and Human Services (1989–93) (endorsed Hillary Clinton)
- **Christine Todd Whitman,** Administrator of the Environmental Protection Agency (2001–03); Governor of New Jersey (1994–2001) (endorsed Hillary Clinton)
- **Robert Zoellick,** United States Deputy Secretary of State (2005–06); U.S. Trade Representative (2001–05); President of the World Bank Group (2007–12)

Governors--As of 2016

- **John Kasich,** Ohio (2011-present)
- **Charlie Baker,** Massachusetts (2015–present)
- **Robert J. Bentley,** Alabama (2011–2017)
- **Dennis Daugaard,** South Dakota (2011–present)
- **Bill Haslam,** Tennessee (2011–present)
- **Gary Herbert,** Utah (2009–present)
- **Larry Hogan,** Maryland (2015–present)
- **Susana Martinez,** New Mexico (2011–present); Chair of the Republican Governors Association (2015–present
- **Bruce Rauner,** Illinois (2015–present)

- **Brian Sandoval,** Nevada (2011–present)
- **Rick Snyder,** Michigan (2011–present)

Former Governors

- **Arne Carlson,** Minnesota (1991–99) (endorsed Hillary Clinton)
- **A. Linwood Holton Jr.,** Virginia (1970–74); Assistant Secretary of State for Legislative Affairs (1974–75) (endorsed Hillary Clinton)
- **Jon Huntsman Jr.,** Governor of Utah (2005–09); United States Ambassador to Russia (2017-); United States Ambassador to China (2009–11); United States Ambassador to Singapore (1992–93)
- **William Milliken,** Michigan (1969–83) (endorsed Hillary Clinton)
- **Kay A. Orr,** Nebraska (1987–91)
- **Tim Pawlenty,** Minnesota (2003–11)
- **Marc Racicot,** Montana (1993–01); Chair of the Republican National Committee (2001–03)
- **Mitt Romney,** Massachusetts (2003–07), 2012 nominee for President
- **Arnold Schwarzenegger,** California (2003–11)
- **William Weld,** Massachusetts (1991–97) (2016 Libertarian nominee for Vice President)
- **Christine Todd Whitman,** New Jersey (1994-2001) **U.S. Senators**

Current State Senators

- **Susan Collins,** Maine (1997–present) (supported Mike Pence for Vice President; presidential vote unknown)
- **Jeff Flake,** Arizona (2013–present) (voted for Evan McMullin)
- **Cory Gardner,** Colorado (2015–present) (wrote-in Mike Pence)
- **Lindsey Graham,** South Carolina (2003–present) (voted for Evan McMullin)
- **Dean Heller,** Nevada (2011–present)
- **Mike Lee, Utah** (2011–present) (voted for Evan McMullin)
- **John McCain,** Arizona (1987–present); 2008 nominee for President.
- **Lisa Murkowski,** Alaska (2002–present)
- **Rob Portman, Ohio (2010-present);** United States Trade Representative (2005–06), Director of the Office of Management and Budget (2006–07) (wrote-in Mike Pence)
- **Ben Sasse,** Nebraska (2015–present)
- **Dan Sullivan,** Alaska (2015–present) (wrote in Mike Pence)

Former State Senators

- **Kelly Ayotte, New Hampshire** (2011–17) (wrote in Mike Pence) [was a current senator on Election Day]
- **Mark Kirk,** Illinois (2010–17) (wrote-in Colin Powell) [was a current senator on Election Day]
- **Norm Coleman,** Minnesota (2003–09)
- **David Durenberger,** Minnesota (1978–95) (endorsed Hillary Clinton) Slade Gorton, Washington (1981–87, 1989–2001) (endorsed Evan McMullin)
- **Gordon J. Humphrey,** New Hampshire (1979–90) (endorsed Hillary Clinton)

- **John Warner, Virginia** (1979–2009); <u>United States Secretary of the Navy</u> (1972–74) (endorsed Hillary Clinton)

Current U.S. Representatives

- **Justin Amash,** Michigan (2011–present)
- **Mike Coffman,** Colorado (2009–present)
- **Barbara Comstock,** Virginia (2015–present)
- **Carlos Curbelo,** Florida (2015–present)
- **Rodney Davis,** Illinois (2013–present)
- **Charlie Dent,** Pennsylvania (2005–present)
- **Bob Dold,** Illinois (2011–13, 2015–17)
- **Jeff Fortenberry,** Nebraska (2005–present)
- **Kay Granger,** Texas (1997–present)
- **Richard L. Hanna,** New York (2011–17) (endorsed Hillary Clinton) Cresent Hardy Nevada (2015–17)
- **Joe Heck,** Nevada (2011–17); 2016 nominee for U.S. Senate
- **Jaime Herrera Beutler,** Washington (2011–present) (writing-in Paul Ryan)
- **Will Hurd,** Texas (2015–present)
- **David Jolly,** Florida (2014–17)
- **John Katko,** New York (2015–present)
- **Adam Kinzinger,** Illinois (2011–present)
- **Steve Knight,** California (2015–present)
- **Frank LoBiondo,** New Jersey (1995–present) (writing-in Mike Pence)
- **Mia Love,** Utah (2015–present)
- **Pat Meehan,** Pennsylvania (2011–present)
- **Erik Paulsen,** Minnesota (2009–present)
- **Reid Ribble,** Wisconsin (2011–17)
- **Scott Rigell,** Virginia (2011–17) (endorsed Gary Johnson)
- **Martha Roby,** Alabama (2011–present)
- **Tom Rooney,** Florida (2009–present)
- **Ileana Ros-Lehtinen,** Florida (1989–present)
- **Mike Simpson,** Idaho (1999–present)
- **Fred Upton,** Michigan (1987–present)
- **David Valadao,** California (2013–present)
- **Ann Wagner,** Missouri (2013–present)

Former U.S. Representatives

- **Steve Bartlett,** Texas (1983–91)
- **Bob Bauman,** Maryland (1973–81)
- **Sherwood Boehlert,** New York (1993–2007) (endorsed Hillary Clinton)
- **Jack Buechner,** Missouri (1987–91)
- **Tom Campbell,** California (1989–93, 1995–2001) (endorsed Gary Johnson)

- **Bill Clinger,** Pennsylvania (1979–97)
- **Tom Coleman,** Missouri (1976–93)
- **Geoff Davis,** Kentucky (2005–12)
- **Mickey Edwards,** Oklahoma (1977–93)
- **David F. Emery,** Maine (1975–83); Chief Deputy Republican Whip (97th Congress); Deputy Director, US Arms Control and Disarmament Agency (1983-88)
- **Harris Fawell,** Illinois (1985–99)
- **Ed Foreman, Texas** (1963–65, 1969–71)
- **Amo Houghton,** New York (1987–2005)
- **Bob Inglis,** South Carolina (1993–99, 2005–11)
- **Jim Kolbe, Arizona** (1985–2007) (endorsed Gary Johnson)
- **Steve Kuykendall,** California (1999–2001)
- **Jim Leach,** Iowa (1977–2007)
- **Pete McCloskey,** California (1967–83) (Democrat since 2007)
- **Connie Morella,** Maryland (1987–2003) (endorsed Hillary Clinton)
- **Mike Parker,** Mississippi (1989–99); Assistant Secretary of the Army for Civil Works (2001–02)
- **Tom Petri,** Wisconsin (1979–2015)
- **John Porter,** Illinois (1980–2001)
- **Joe Scarborough,** Florida (1995–2001); commentator and author)
- **Claudine Schneider,** Rhode Island (1981–91) (endorsed Hillary Clinton)
- **Chris Shays,** Connecticut (1987–2009) (endorsed Hillary Clinton)
- **Peter Smith,** Vermont (1989–1991)
- **Mark Souder,** Indiana (1995–2010)
- **J.C. Watts,** Oklahoma (1995–2003)
- **Edward Weber,** Ohio (1981–83)
- **Vin Weber,** Minnesota (1983–93)
- **G. William Whitehurst,** Virginia (1969–87)
- **Dick Zimmer,** New Jersey (1991–97) (endorsed Gary Johnson)

Former State Department officials

- **Richard Armitage,** Deputy Secretary of State; Assistant Secretary of Defense for International Security Affairs (endorsed Hillary Clinton)
- **John B. Bellinger III,** Legal Adviser of the Department of State; Legal Adviser to the National Security Council)
- **Robert Blackwill,** United States Ambassador to India; Deputy National Security Advisor for Strategic Planning (endorsed Hillary Clinton)
- **R. Nicholas Burns,** Under Secretary of State for Political Affairs; United States Ambassador to NATO; United States Ambassador to Greece (endorsed Hillary Clinton)
- **Eliot A. Cohen,** Counselor of the United States Department of State
- **Chester Crocker**, Assistant Secretary of State for African Affairs
- **Jendayi Frazer,** Assistant Secretary of State for African Affairs
- **James K. Glassman,** Under Secretary of State for Public Diplomacy and Public Affairs (endorsed Hillary Clinton)

- **David F. Gordon,** Director of Policy Planning
- **Donald Gregg,** United States Ambassador to South Korea
- **David A. Gross,** U.S. Coordinator for International Communications and Information Policy (endorsed Hillary Clinton)
- **John Hillen,** Assistant Secretary of State for Political-Military Affairs
- Reuben Jeffery III, Under Secretary of State for Economic Growth, Energy, and the Environment
- **Robert Joseph,** Under Secretary of State for Arms Control and International Security Affairs
- David J. Kramer, Assistant Secretary of State for Democracy, Human Rights, and Labor
- **Stephen D. Krasner,** Director of Policy Planning
- Frank Lavin, United States Ambassador to Singapore; Under Secretary of Commerce for International Trade (endorsed Hillary Clinton)
- **Robert McCallum,** United States Ambassador to Australia; Acting United States Deputy Attorney General
- **Richard Miles,** United States Ambassador to Azerbaijan, Bulgaria, and Georgia; Acting United States Ambassador to Kyrgyzstan
- **Roger Noriega,** Assistant Secretary of State for Western Hemisphere Affairs
- **John Osborn,** Member of the U.S. Advisory Commission on Public Diplomacy
- **Kristen Silverberg,** Assistant Secretary of State for International Organization Affairs
- **William Howard Taft IV,** Legal Adviser of the Department of State; United States Ambassador to NATO; United States Deputy Secretary of Defense
- **Shirin R. Tahir-Kheli,** Senior Advisor for Women's Empowerment; Special Assistant to the President for Democracy, Human Rights and International Operations (endorsed Hillary Clinton)
- **Betty Tamposi,** Assistant Secretary of State for Consular Affairs (endorsed Hillary Clinton)
- **Peter Teeley,** United States Ambassador to Canada (endorsed Hillary Clinton)
- **Robert Tuttle,** United States Ambassador to the United Kingdom (endorsed Hillary Clinton)
- **Philip Zelikow,** Counselor of the United States Department of State

Former Defense Department Officials

- **Don Bacon,** Brigadier General, <u>United States Air Force</u>; Representative for <u>Nebraska's 2nd district</u>
- **Seth Cropsey,** Assistant Secretary of Defense for Special Operations/Low Intensity Conflict & Interdependent Capabilities
- Michael B. Donley, United States Secretary of the Air Force (endorsed Hillary Clinton)
- **Eric Edelman,** Under Secretary of Defense for Policy
- **Doug Feith,** Under Secretary of Defense for Policy
- **Robert Hastings,** Acting Assistant to the Secretary of Defense for Public Affairs
- **Tim Kane,** United States Air Force intelligence officer; Chief Labor Economist, Joint Economic Committee
- **Mary Beth Long,** Assistant Secretary of Defense for International Security Affairs
- **Alberto J. Mora,** General Counsel of the Navy (endorsed Hillary Clinton)
- Gale Pollock, Acting Surgeon General of the United States Army (endorsed Hillary Clinton)
- **Martha Rainville,** Major General, United States Air Force; Vermont Adjutant General
- **Michael Rubin,** Defense Country Director for Iran and Iraq
- **Kalev Sepp,** Deputy Assistant Secretary of Defense for Special Operations Capabilities

- **Matthew Waxman,** Deputy Assistant Secretary of Defense for Detainee Affairs (endorsed Hillary Clinton)
- **Paul Wolfowitz,** United States Deputy Secretary of Defense; President of the World Bank Group
- **Dov Zakheim,** Comptroller of the Department of Defense

Former National Security Officials

- **Ken Adelman,** Director of the Arms Control and Disarmament Agency (endorsed Hillary Clinton)
- **Mike Baker, Covert Operations Officer,** Central Intelligence Agency
- **Tom Donnelly, Director of the Policy Group,** House Armed Services Committee
- **Gary Edson,** Deputy National Security Advisor
- Richard Falkenrath, Deputy Homeland Security Advisor
- **Peter Feaver,** Senior Director for Strategic Planning
- **Aaron Friedberg,** Deputy National Security Advisor to the Vice President
- **Greg Garcia,** Assistant Secretary of Homeland Security for Cyber Security and Telecommunications[]
- **Michael Green, Senior Director for Asia,** National Security Council
- **Paul Haenle, Director for China and Taiwan,** National Security Council
- **Michael Hayden,** Director of the Central Intelligence Agency (2006–09)
- **William Inboden,** Senior Director for Strategic Planning, National Security Council
- **James Jeffrey,** Deputy National Security Advisor
- **James C. Langdon, Jr.,** Chair of the President's Intelligence Advisory Board
- **Deborah Loewer,** Director of the White House Situation Room (endorsed Hillary Clinton)
- **Evan McMullin,** Operations Officer, Central Intelligence Agency; Senior Adviser for National Security, House Foreign Affairs Committee (Independent candidate for President)
- **Paul D. Miller,** Director for Afghanistan, National Security Council[
- **Meghan O'Sullivan,** Deputy National Security Advisor for Iraq and Afghanistan
- **Kori Schake, Director of Defense Strategy,** National Security Council
- **Gary Schmitt, Executive Director of the** President's Intelligence Advisory Board
- **Brent Scowcroft,** National Security Advisor (1975–77, 1989–93); Chair of the President's Intelligence Advisory Board (2001–05) (endorsed Hillary Clinton)
- **David Shedd,** Deputy Director of National Intelligence; Acting Director of the Defense Intelligence Agency
- **Stephen Slick,** Senior Director for Intelligence Programs, National Security Council
- **Frances Townsend,** Homeland Security Advisor
- **Kenneth Wainstein,** Homeland Security Advisor

Other former federal government officials

- **Donald B. Ayer,** United States Deputy Attorney General
- **Phillip D. Brady,** White House Staff Secretary; White House Cabinet Secretary (endorsed Hillary Clinton)
- **Paul K. Charlton,** United States Attorney

- **Linda Chavez,** Director of the Office of Public Liaison; 1986 nominee for U.S. Senator from Maryland
- **Jim Cicconi,** White House Staff Secretary (endorsed Hillary Clinton)
- **Scott Evertz,** Director of the Office of National AIDS Policy (endorsed Hillary Clinton
- **Tony Fratto,** Deputy White House Press Secretary
- **Charles Fried,** United States Solicitor General; Associate Justice of the Massachusetts Supreme Judicial Court (endorsed Hillary Clinton)
- **Fred T. Goldberg, Jr.,** Assistant Secretary of the Treasury for Tax Policy; Commissioner of Internal Revenue (endorsed Hillary Clinton)
- **Theodore Kassinger,** United States Deputy Secretary of Commerce
- Bill Kristol, Chief of Staff to the Vice President (endorsed Evan McMullin)
- **Thomas Mallon,** Deputy Chairman of the National Endowment for the Humanities
- **Rosario Marin,** Treasurer of the United States (endorsed Hillary Clinton)
- **John McKay,** former United States Attorney (endorsed Hillary Clinton)
- **Andrew Natsios,** Administrator of the United States Agency for International Development; Chair of the Massachusetts Republican Party
- **Daniel F. Runde,** Director of the Global Development Alliance
- Larry D. Thompson, United States Deputy Attorney General
- **Dan Webb, former** United States Attorney (endorsed Hillary Clinton)
- **Peter Wehner,** Director of the Office of Strategic Initiatives
- **Lezlee Westine,** Director of the Office of Public Liaison (2001–2005) (endorsed Hillary Clinton)
- **Peter Zeidenberg,** Assistant United States Attorney

Current State Officials

- **Brian Calley,** Lieutenant Governor of Michigan (2011–present)
- **Spencer Cox,** Lieutenant Governor of Utah (2013–present)
- **Kim Guadagno,** Lieutenant Governor of New Jersey (2010–present)

Former State Officials

- **Paul Anderson,** Associate Justice of the Minnesota Supreme Court (1994–2013) (endorsed Hillary Clinton)
- **Greg Bell,** Lieutenant Governor of Utah (2009–13) (endorsed Evan McMullin) Bob Brown, Secretary of State of Montana (2001–05) (endorsed Hillary Clinton
- **Betty Montgomery,** Attorney General of Ohio (1995–2003), Ohio State Auditor (2003–07)
- **Sam Reed,** Secretary of State of Washington (2000–12) (endorsed Evan McMullin) **Mark Shurtleff, Attorney General of Utah (2001–13) (endorsed Hillary Clinton)**
- **Robert Smith,** Associate Judge of the New York Court of Appeals (2004–14) (endorsed Hillary Clinton)
- **Michael Steele,** Lieutenant Governor of Maryland (2003–07) and RNC Chair (2009–11)
- **Diana Taylor,** New York Superintendent of Banks (2003–07) (endorsed Hillary Clinton
- **Grant Woods,** Attorney General of Arizona (1991–99) (endorsed Hillary Clinton)

Current State Legislators

- **Rocky Chavez,** California State Representative (2012–present)
- **Jack Ciattarelli,** New Jersey State Representative (2011–present)
- **Neal Collins,** South Carolina State Representative (2014–present)
- **Kurt Daudt Minnesota State Representative** (2011–present), Speaker of the Minnesota House of Representatives (2015–present)
- **David Johnson,** Iowa State Senator (2003–present)
- **Mark B. Madsen,** Utah State Senator (2005–present) (endorsed Gary Johnson)
- **Chad Mayes,** California State Assembly Minority Leader (2014–present)
- **Charisse Millett,** Alaska State Representative (2009–present), Majority Leader (2015–present)
- **Ross Spano,** Florida State Representative (2012–present)
- **Joe Sweeney,** New Hampshire State Representative (2012–present)

Former State Legislators

- **Michael Balboni,** New York State Senator (1998–2007) (endorsed Hillary Clinton)
- **Lois Sherman Hagarty,** Pennsylvania State Representative (1980–92)
- **Brian Lees,** Massachusetts State Senator (1989–2007), Minority Leader (1993–2007)
- **Jack McGregor,** Pennsylvania State Senator (1963–70) (endorsed Hillary Clinton)
- **Will Weatherford,** Florida State Representative (2006–14), Speaker of the Florida House of Representatives (2012–14)

Municipal Officials

- **Joel Giambra,** former Erie County Executive (endorsed Hillary Clinton)
- **Carlos A. Giménez,** Mayor of Miami-Dade County (endorsed Hillary Clinton)
- **Danny Jones,** Mayor of Charleston, West Virginia (endorsed Gary Johnson)
- **Aimee Winder Newton,** Member of the Salt Lake County Council
- **Tomás Regalado,** Mayor of Miami

Other notable individuals
Republican Party figures

- **Laura Bush,** former First Lady of the United States
- **Ben Shapiro,** conservative commentator
- **George Will,** conservative commentator
- **Steve Baer,** former President, United Republican Fund of Illinois
- **Max Boot,** author (endorsed Hillary Clinton)
- **Ellen Bork,** political consultant
- **Laura Bush,** First Lady of the United States (2001–09); First Lady of Texas (1995–2000)
- **Marvin Bush,** son of George H. W. Bush, brother of George W. Bush and Jeb Bush (endorsed Gary Johnson)
- **Al Cardenas,** former chair of the Republican Party of Florida

- **Patrick Chovanec,** economist
- **Beau Correll,** attorney, political activist (led Free The Delegates movement, filed successful federal lawsuit to unbind delegates)
- **Mindy Finn,** political consultant, strategist, and activist (Independent running mate for Evan McMullin
- **Darryl Glenn,** 2016 nominee for U.S. Senator from Colorado
- **Juan Hernandez,** political consultant, co-founder of Hispanic Republicans of Texas (endorsed Gary Johnson)
- **Matt Higgins,** former press secretary for New York City Mayor Rudy Giuliani (endorsed Hillary Clinton)
- **Robert Kagan,** former foreign policy advisor and speechwriter (endorsed Hillary Clinton)
- **Matt Kibbe,** libertarian ideals advocate
- **Jimmy LaSalvia,** co-founder of GOProud (endorsed Hillary Clinton)
- **Kevin Madden,** spokesperson for 2012 presidential nominee, Mitt Romney
- **Ken Mehlman,** former Chair of the Republican National Committee
- **Mike Murphy,** political consultant and commentator (endorsed Hillary Clinton)
- **Patrick Ruffini,** political strategist
- **Mark Salter,** chief aide to John McCain (endorsed Hillary Clinton)
- **Randy Scheunemann,** national security and foreign policy advisor
- **Steve Schmidt,** campaign strategist
- **Gabriel Schoenfeld,** former Senior Advisor to 2012 presidential nominee Mitt Romney
- **Lionel Sosa,** political consultant (endorsed Hillary Clinton)
- **A. J. Spiker,** Chair of the Iowa Republican Party
- **Stuart Stevens,** political consultant and strategist
- **Mac Stipanovich,** strategist and lobbyist; former Chief of Staff to Bob Martinez (endorsed Hillary Clinton)
- **John Weaver,** strategist
- **Rick Wilson,** political consultant and former Republican strategist.

Conservative Academics, Journalists and Commentators

- **Michael Auslin,** Resident Scholar and Director of Japanese Studies at the American Enterprise Institute
- **Glenn Beck,** former Fox News host, radio host, columnist, and author (endorsed Darrell Castle)
- **Guy Benson,** journalist
- **Michael Berry,** radio host
- **L. Brent Bozell III,** activist and writer
- **David Brooks,** columnist
- **Christine Caine,** evangelical author
- **Steven G. Calabresi,** legal scholar and co-founder of the Federalist Society
- **Mona Charen,** columnist and author
- **Lanhee Chen,** academic and commentator
- **Joshua Claybourn,** attorney, author, and former convention delegate
- **Ross Douthat,** columnist

- **Daniel W. Drezner,** blogger
- **Richard Epstein,** legal scholar
- **Erick Erickson,** blogger (endorsed Evan McMullin)
- **Niall Ferguson,** professor of history
- **David A. French,** author and journalist
- **David Frum,** columnist and speechwriter for George W. Bush (voted for Hillary Clinton)
- **Jeffrey Gedmin,** author
- **Robert P. George,** academic
- **Reuel Marc Gerecht,** writer (endorsed Hillary Clinton)
- **Michael Gerson,** columnist and speechwriter for George W. Bush
- **Jonah Goldberg,** columnist and author (endorsed Evan McMullin)
- **Michael Graham,** radio host
- **Mary R. Habeck,** professor of strategic studies
- **David Harsanyi,** columnist
- **Stephen F. Hayes,** columnist
- **Quin Hillyer,** columnist
- **Margaret Hoover,** consultant and commentator
- **Charles Krauthammer,** columnist (wrote in Paul Ryan or Ben Sasse)
- **Matt K. Lewis,** columnist and commentator
- **Dana Loesch,** author and commentator
- **Peter Mansoor,** military historian (endorsed Hillary Clinton)
- **Meghan McCain**, commentator, daughter of Senator John McCain (voted for Evan McMullin)
- **Beth Moore,** evangelical author
- **Russell D. Moore,** evangelical theologian, head of the Southern Baptist Convention's Ethics and Religious Liberty Commission (writing-in Ben Sasse)
- **Charles Murray,** political scientist and commentator
- **Ana Navarro,** strategist and commentator (voted for Hillary Clinton)
- **Tom Nichols,** national security affairs scholar (endorsed Hillary Clinton)
- **John Noonan,** national security analyst and commentator
- **Marvin Olasky,** editor-in-chief of World
- **Mackubin Thomas Owens,** national security advisor
- **Katie Pavlich,** journalist
- **Daniel Pipes,** historian and columnist
- **Danielle Pletka,** foreign policy writer
- **John Podhoretz,** writer and columnist
- **Dorothy Rabinowitz,** journalist (endorsed Hillary Clinton)
- **Jennifer Rubin,** journalist
- **Ben Shapiro,** columnist and commentator
- **Bret Stephens,** journalist (voted for Hillary Clinton)
- **Charlie Sykes,** author, radio host, MSNBC commentator
- **Ray Takeyh,** Senior Fellow at the Council on Foreign Relations
- **Ruth Wedgwood,** professor of international law and diplomacy
- **Jamie Weinstein,** political journalist
- **Montel Williams,** talk show host and commentator

- **George Will,** columnist
- **Kevin D. Williamson,** writer

Business leaders

- **Daniel Akerson,** former Chairman and CEO of General Motors (endorsed Hillary Clinton)
- **Marc Andreessen,** co-founder of Netscape; founder of Andreessen Horowitz (endorsed Hillary Clinton) Mike Fernandez, founder of MBF Healthcare Partners (endorsed Hillary Clinton)
- **Seth Klarman,** founder of Baupost Group (endorsed Hillary Clinton)
- **Hamid R. Moghadam,** CEO of Prologis (endorsed Hillary Clinton)
- **James Murren,** Chairman and CEO of MGM Resorts International (endorsed Hillary Clinton)
- **Chuck Robbins,** CEO of Cisco Systems (endorsed Hillary Clinton)
- **Paul Singer,** founder and CEO of Elliott Management Corporation
- **Harry E. Sloan,** former CEO of Metro-Goldwyn-Mayer (endorsed Hillary Clinton)
- **Jack Welch,** former CEO of General Electric
- **Meg Whitman,** CEO of Hewlett Packard Enterprise; former CEO of eBay; 2010 California nominee for Governor of California (endorsed Hillary Clinton)

Republican Groups

- **Harvard Republican Club**
- **Penn State College Republicans**
- **Kenyon Republicans**
- **The University of the South College Republicans**
- **Cornell Republicans** (endorsed Gary Johnson)
- **New Mexico College Republicans** (endorsed Gary Johnson)
- **Log Cabin Republicans**

Stop Trump Movement

- **Protests against Donald Trump**
- **List of Donald Trump presidential campaign endorsements,** 2016
- **List of Hillary Clinton presidential campaign political endorsements,** 2016
- **List of Hillary Clinton presidential campaign non-political endorsements,** 2016
- **Democratic opposition to Hillary Clinton in 2016**
- **List of Evan McMullin presidential campaign endorsements,** 2016
- **List of Gary Johnson presidential campaign endorsements,** 2016
- **List of Jill Stein presidential campaign endorsements,** 2016
- **Newspaper endorsements in the United States presidential election,** 2016

Who Voted for Trump vs Clinton?

According to *Boston Globe,* 2016 exit poll demographics showed:

Voter Breakdown	%	Clinton	%	Trump	%
Sex: Men	48		41		53
Women	52		54		42
White	70		37		58
Race: Black	12		88		8
Hispanic	11		65		29
Asian	4		65		29
Other	3		57		37
Age: 8–29	19		54		37
30–44	25		50		42
45–64	40		44		53
65+	16		45		52
Income: < $50,000	36		52		41
> $50,000	64		47		49
Education by Race: White/College Grad	37		45		49
White/Not College Grad	34		28		67
Nonwhite/College Grad	13		71		23
Nonwhite/Not College Grad	16		75		20

CHAPTER FIVE: UNITED WE DO NOT STAND

If you ask Trump whether he's racist, he has a standard response: He claims that no, in fact, he's "the least racist person that you've ever encountered." His actions proved the opposite.

Travel Ban. The first version of the travel ban, which clearly centered on Muslim-majority countries, led to a rise of hate and bigotry, which may have already been brewing. This became very clear in August at the Unite to Right rally in Charlottesville, where the ultra-right hoped to recreate the marches of Hitler Youth in the 1930s. The white nationalists paraded down the streets with their torches, which riled up the counter-protesters. The neo-Nazis, shouting "Blood and soil! You will not replace us! Jews will not replace us!", stopped at the Thomas Jefferson statue. Protesters and counter-protesters met face-to-face and fighting ensued. The police did not arrive until the skirmishes were underway.

The situation worsened the next day, as people arrived with guns, shields and clubs. When a state of emergency was declared, it seemed that the worst situation was averted. Then, James Alex Fields, Jr. drove his car into a crowd of pedestrians , reversed and did the same into another group. One woman was killed and 19 others were injured. Trump's comments following this horrible event divided the country even more than this protest. He tweeted about the event, "We ALL must be united & condemn all that hate stands for. There is no place for this kind of violence in America. Lets come together as one!"

In a follow-up speech, he added, "We condemn in the strongest possible terms this egregious display of hatred, bigotry, and violence on many sides — on many sides. It's been going on for a long time in our country, not Donald Trump, not Barack Obama, it's been going on for a long, long time."

The President ignored reporters who asked him to denounce white nationalists or to say whether he considered the events terrorism. Democrats and Republicans both criticized his lack of using such terms as "neo-Nazi," "white supremacy" or "white nationalism." At a Phoenix rally a couple of days later, he strongly defended his comments but left out his comments about "both sides." Public figures in Israel, Germany, and the United Kingdom condemned Trump for his remarks and not differentiating between the groups meeting at the rally.

Monuments.. Denouncing removal of Confederate statues, Trump called the actions "sad" and "foolish." He added, "Bad...to see history and culture of our great country being ripped apart with the removal of our beautiful statues and monuments. You can't change history, but you can learn from it. He then questioned whether such figures as President Washington would be next. "So foolish!"

Nigeria. Right after his election, Trump became very angry after seeing a list of foreigners who were granted visas to enter the U.S. in 2017, 40,000 of whom were Nigerians. According to officials present at the meeting, he said that once they see America, they'll never "go back to their huts" in Africa.

Haiti. Trump also had negative comments about the 15,000 Haitians who came to the U.S. "They all have AIDS," he declared.

El Salvador, Haiti, El Salvador and Other African Nations. These countries received another huge slam at the end of Trump's first year in office. The President called them "shithole countries," when talking with a bipartisan group about immigration.

Senator Lindsey Graham, who made several negative remarks about Trump during the election but later became one of his golfing buddies, lost points when confronting the President at this bipartisan meeting. Graham apparently "said his piece" after Trump's strong anti-Haiti and African comments. "The President and all those attending the meeting   know what I said and how I feel," explained Graham.

Scandinavia. If using such language was not bad enough, Trump added that there should be more people coming from Scandinavian nations such as Norway. Ironically, this comment about Norway came only a few days after the White House issued an official schedule for the President, which included "Normay" instead of "Norway." This was one of numerous spelling errors from the White House.

African-American Football Players.. Trump ranted against Stephen Curry and other "son of a bitch" N.F.L. players who chose to "disrespect" the "Flag (or Country)," as Trump tweeted, by kneeling during the national anthem. Trump's strong words against these football players was blatantly racist. He raved about fans who booed some of these protesting athletes and claimed that his criticism had "nothing to do with race."

Native Americans.. Trump derogatorily referred to Senator Elizabeth Warren as "Pocahontas,." as he did during election rallies. At an event honoring Native American Code Talkers who served in World War II, Trump said, "You were here long before any of us were here. Although we have a representative in Congress who they say was here a long time ago. They call her Pocahontas." Turning to the veterans, Trump said, "but do you know what? I like you."

"This was supposed to be an event to honor heroes, people who put it all on the line for our country," Warren said. "It is deeply unfortunate that the President of the United States can't even make it through a ceremony honoring these heroes without throwing out a racial slur."

Asians 1. In January 2018, Trump commented about a "pretty Korean lady" who attended an Oval Office briefing. This woman apparently was an expert in hostage negotiations, who was presenting information about an impending release of a family held in Pakistan. Trump proceeded to ask her where she was from, to which she answered "New York." He was reportedly not satisfied with the answer and asked her the same question again, so she said "Manhattan."

Trump asked where her "people" were from. The analyst then said her parents were from South Korea. The President finally asked a nearby adviser why that "pretty Korean lady" was not leading negotiations with North Korea on behalf of the White House. Her position had nothing to do with North Korean negotiations.

<u>Asians 2</u>. During a speech in Missouri to promote the GOP tax bill, Trump made fun of leaders he had met during his recent Asian trip. While explaining that he had advised several leaders on how to boost their defense spending, Trump proceeded to imitate the leaders: He hunched his shoulders and looked around the room wide-eyed in a mocking gesture to imply that these officials did not understand his words.

<u>Puerto Rico.</u> Although Trump learned that Puerto Rico was part of the U.S., this did not mean that these citizens had equal billing with Texas and Florida after devastating hurricanes. Trump's "racist neglect of Puerto Rico could cost lives after the massive devastation caused by Hurricane Mari," tweeted a former Hillary Clinton aide. It took two days before the President responded to the islands' needs, but not in the most caring way. Tossing rolls of paper towels into the surrounding crowd, Trump later explained, "They had these beautiful, soft towels. Very good towels...And I came in and there was a crowd of a lot of people. And they were screaming and they were loving everything. I was having fun, they were having fun . They said 'Throw 'em to me! Throw 'em to me, Mr. President!'"

San Juan Mayor Carmen Yulin Cruz said, "He's treating Puerto Rico different than the U.S. treated Haiti. For some reason, he's taking out all his anger on Puerto Rico." She added,

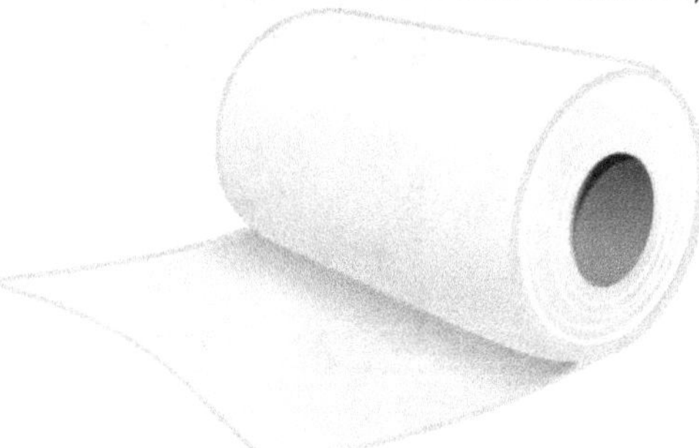

"There's a big disconnect between the big heart of the volunteers and the people that are here working on the ground and, frankly, the big mouth of the President of the United States that continues to add insult to injury."

(It is not only Trump, but his cabinet members who are failing to remember the equal rights amendment. Secretary DeVos spent her first year in the Trump Administration trying her best to weaken civil rights protection. Her first act as Secretary was to rescind guidance concerning a school's obligation to protect transgender students. She did away with numerous guidance documents that detailed the rights of disabled students and withdrew guidance on campus sexual violence that makes it more difficult for survivors to get justice due. In March 2018, she spoke in front of a Congressional committee regarding the potential withdrawal of critical guidelines that protect students of color from discrimination in school discipline.)

CHAPTER SIX: FOREIGN FOREIGN AFFAIRS

Since Trump was elected, the political situation in the U.S. has become of considerable interest to countries worldwide. Everyone has been trying to decipher his tweets and actions both nationally and globally. Considering his lack of knowledge about foreign affairs, this is understandable. Here are some of his most bizarre foreign relations.

Australia. Trump was only in his first week as President when he called Australian Prime Minister Malcolm Turnbull. He quickly succeeded in disturbing a long-time American ally by. boasting about his win and then ranting about Obama's decision to accept a few refugees who were trying to enter Australia. Trump did not understand the arrangement between the two countries; he was only upset that this was something that the Obama Administration had decided. Turnbull tried to explain, to no avail.

According to the phone call's transcript, Trump rudely said to the Prime Minister, "I have had it. I have been making these calls all day and this is the most unpleasant call all day. Putin was a pleasant call. This is ridiculous." He then ended the conversation after only 25 minutes into what was expected to be an hour-long call.

Mexico. Speaking of bad relations... President Enrique Peña Nieto and Trump phone in January. Trump said that Nieto press that Mexico was unwilling to pay for are going to say that Mexico is not going to then I do not want to meet with you guys because I cannot live with that," Trump

Mexican also spoke by could not tell the the wall. "If you pay for the wall, anymore, ended up saying.

Montenegro. When Trump attended his first NATO summit, he blamed the leaders for not spending enough on defense. Later, when everyone gathered to take a group photograph, Trump forged ahead of the pack. He grabbed Montenegro Prime Minister Dusko Markovic by the arm, pushed him out of the way, and took the lead position . He then adjusted his suit jacket to look unruffled.

France 1. Instead of saying something politically correct to the wife of French President Macron when the two of them met, Trump reverted to his sexist ways by saying, "You're in such good shape!" while physically appraising her. He then turned to Macron and repeated, "She's in such good physical shape. Beautiful."

France 2. After deadly terrorist attacks in Nice and Paris, Trump suggested that France's capital had lost its identity. "Take a look at what's happened in France. I have a friend; he's a very, very substantial guy. He loves the city of lights. He loves Paris. And I said, 'Jim, let me ask you a question. How's Paris doing?' [To which he replied:] 'Paris? I don't go there anymore. Paris is no longer Paris.'" Of course, "Jim" did not exist, and Trump made this whole story up.

<u>Germany</u>. A photo-op at a meeting in the Oval Office between German Chancellor Angela Merkel and Trump ended on a slightly strained note. Photographers snapped photos of the two leaders, who were seated. The photographers then called out "Handshake" in order to get the obligatory photo of the two shaking hands. Trump did not respond, but. Merkel could be heard saying something to him about a handshake. However, it was noisy in the room; perhaps the President did not hear her, and it was just one of those passing things.

When asked about the incident, Trump retorted: "Yeah well, believe it or not I have a great relationship with Chancellor Merkel. They come up with this thing about shaking hands -- I shook her hand four times before I sat down -- and it turns out that either a reporter or somebody said, shake her hand. I never heard it, but I would have been glad to shake ... and they made the shaking of the hands ... a big deal."

At a later time when asked about his relationship with Merkel he responded, They would not have a good one "because, um, I'm at odds on, you know, the NATO payments and I'm at odds on immigration. We had unbelievable chemistry. And people have given me credit for having great chemistry with all of the leaders."

Meanwhile, at the NATO summit when several world leaders were unable to reach an agreement on climate change with Trump, the Associated Press reported that Merkel said, "The times in which we can fully count on others are somewhat over, as I have experienced in the past few days."

<u>United Kingdom 1</u>. After a terror attack in London, which killed 7 and wounded 48, Trump blasted Muslim London Mayor Sadiq Khan. Khan had gone on television to encourage Londoners to stand strong when facing terror and not be frightened by the additional police presence. Erroneously seeing this as being flippant, Trump tweeted sarcastically, "At least 7 dead and 48 wounded in terror attack, and Mayor of London says there is 'no reason to be alarmed!'"

<u>United Kingdom 2</u>. Officials in Great Britain were not pleased that Trump was coming for a visit. In fact, Parliament was not successful in its vote to take back the nation's invitation. Trump apparently heard the message loud and clear. He called off his trip to London to open the new American embassy. He even expressed wrong information about this earlier intended trip. He incorrectly blamed Obama for "selling off "perhaps the best located and finest embassy in London for 'peanuts.'"

"Reason I canceled my trip to London is that I am not a big fan of the Obama Administration having sold perhaps the best located and finest embassy in London for "peanuts," only to build a new one in an off location for 1.2 billion dollars. Bad deal. Wanted me to cut ribbon-NO!," read his tweet.

Actually, U.S. diplomats had discussed relocating the U.S. embassy as early as 2003, because this property was not adequately equipped to handle new security threats. The building was put up for sale in October 2008, eight days before Obama won his first Presidential election.

<u>Egypt</u>. When Trump met dictator Egyptian President Abdel Fattah el-Sisi, the latter complimented the President on his "unique personality that is capable of doing the impossible."

A few minutes later, Trump returned the compliment by saying something nice about el-Sisi's shoes. "Love your shoes. Boy, those shoes. Man..."

Dictators 1.. The number of journalists jailed for disseminating "fake news" hit a new record during 2017. The Committee to Protect Journalists (CPJ) condemned Trump for celebrating authoritarian leaders. Trump has shown considerable support and respect for dictators, as seen by his relationship with Russia. Similarly, he has praised Turkish President Recep Tayyip Erdogan and Chinese President Xi Jinping, countries where many journalists are jailed for "trumped-up charges" (no pun intended). Turkey has continued to be the worst offender, but Trump called Erdogan his friend who "gets very high marks." Also, the President did not condemn China for its human rights violations, yet he has stated that American journalists are a "stain on America."

CPJ said they believed that Trump's hatred of the media and embrace of authoritarian dictators added to the increase in imprisonment. The organization noted that 262 journalists were imprisoned worldwide for their work. This was a slight increase over the 259 in 2016; this latter number was also the highest since data was first collected in the early 1990s.

Dictators 2. Trump may have signed an Executive Order that strongly condemned human rights violations, but his actions proved differently. During his tour of Asia, Trump did not press the Vietnamese regime on what Human Rights Watch calls a "dire" lack of individual freedoms. After Trump's visit, Senator John McCain tweeted: "@POTUS in #Danang & no mention of human rights - Sad." Trump instead talked about trade and praised the Vietnamese president for doing "an outstanding job."

Then Trump went to Manila where President Rodrigo Duterte had been accused of fighting the drug trade through a campaign of extrajudicial killings. Trump claimed he had a "great relationship" with Duterte and never mentioned human rights at all.

In fact, the White House once had a senior National Security Council post called "Special Assistant to the President for Multilateral Affairs and Human Rights," who coordinated, developed, and helped implement government policy related to human rights and humanitarian relief. Under Trump, the title for this position was changed to "Special Assistant for International Organizations and Alliances," with the words "Human Rights" removed. The person named to the post, Garry Hall, did not have any background or experience in human rights policy.

North Korea. Trump, however, disliked the North Korean leader Kim Jong-un from day one, perhaps because they are so similar in their bullying approach to others. North Korea conducted a series of missile and nuclear tests to demonstrate the nation's ability to launch ballistic missiles beyond its immediate region and that technology was considerably further along than thought. At times the twitter wars became quite unsettling between the two leaders, which heightened fears across the U.S. because of Trump's personality.

"North Korean Leader Kim Jong Un just stated that the 'Nuclear Button is on his desk at all times.' Will someone from his depleted and food starved regime please inform him that I too have a Nuclear Button, but it is a much bigger & more powerful one than his, and my Button works!. Much bigger & more powerful. 'My Button works'"

Japan. It has appeared that Trump and the Japanese Prime Minister Shinzo Abe have gotten along, especially on the golf course. When the two met in November, Trump first complimented the strength of Japan's economy and then added, "I don't know if it's as good as ours. I think not. OK? We're going to try to keep it that way. And you'll be second."

However, just the fact that the two men have played golf together in Florida does not mean they are the best of friends. At the beginning of 2018, Trump voiced dissatisfaction with Japan's automobile safety and environmental standards. During a meeting with U.S. governors, Trump said U.S. automakers sent cars with the best safety and environmental features to Japan but were rejected "after inspections that lasted forever."

China 1. Much to the amazement of U.S. officials, Trump shared Syria's bombing with Chinese President Xi Jinping at Mar-A-Lago. This is how Trump explained it to Fox News: "I was sitting at the table. We had finished dinner. We're now having dessert. And we had the most beautiful piece of chocolate cake that   you've ever seen, and President Xi was enjoying it. And I was given the   message from the generals that the ships are locked and loaded, what do you do? And we make a determination to do it, so the missiles were on the way. And I said, Mr. President, let me explain something to you--this was during dessert--we've just fired 59 missiles, all of which hit, by the way, unbelievable, from, you know, hundreds of miles away, all of which hit, amazing."

China 2. Relationships with China has hanged minute-by-minute, as does everything with Trump. In January, Trump complained repeatedly that China had not done enough to rein in a hostile North Korea. "China has been taking out massive amounts of money & wealth from the U.S. in totally one-sided trade, but won't help with North Korea. Nice!" he tweeted right after his inauguration. Two months later, he reiterated: "North Korea is behaving very badly. They have been 'playing' the United States for years. China has done little to help!"

In April, he hosted President Xi in D.C., when the two "developed a very good relationship," Trump said. Later, when visiting Beijing, Trump said "I don't blame China. After all, who can blame a country for being able to take advantage of another country to the benefit of its citizens."

At the end of 2017, Trump scolded China in one of his Tweets: He said he was "very disappointed" over a report that China is continuing to supply oil to North Korea – since Trump had been playing the bully role with North Korea. "Caught RED HANDED - very disappointed that China is allowing oil to go into North Korea," noted the Tweet. "There will never be a friendly solution to the North Korea problem if this continues to happen!"

Trans-Pacific Partnership (TPP). Only three days into his administration, Trump withdrew from negotiations for the TPP. Many analysts feared that the U.S. withdrawal would spell the end to the whole agreement, but the 11 remaining Pacific Rim countries consented to move forward on their own The remaining bloc said it has a plan to start trading more freely between themselves.

North American Free Trade Agreement (NAFTA).. While running for President, Trump called NAFTA "the worst trade deal" ever signed by the U.S. He has blamed this agreement for erasing U.S. manufacturing jobs because it allowed companies to move factories to Mexico where labor is cheaper. Trump continued to oscillate about NAFTA. In his first 100 days, he threatened to withdraw from the agreement if Canada and Mexico did not agree to renegotiate. They consented to talk, since they saw the agreement as outdated. By November, the fifth round of negotiations began between the three countries, and discussions continued into 2018.

If Trump ended NAFTA without Congress' approval, tariffs could benefit U.S. oil companies by raising prices on imported Mexican oil and restoring the one-half to three-quarters million manufacturing jobs lost in states such as California and Michigan. On the other hand, tariffs would raise the price of imports for American consumers. U.S. farmers have been worried this could impact their work by losing billions of dollars of agricultural products. Further, tourism, agriculture, automotives and national security could be negatively impacted. At the beginning of 2018, House Republicans on Tuesday called on President Trump to update NAFTA while urging caution on slapping tariffs on imports.

Cuba. Trump announced a partial rollback of the Obama Administration's reconciliation with Cuba. Since thist had Obama's name on it, Trump's decision came as no surprise. Under the new guidelines, the U.S. reinstated restrictions on travel and trade with Cuba without severing diplomatic ties. In September, Trump reduced the U.S. embassy staff in Havana by half.

Iran. After much deliberation, the President announced he would not recertify Iran's compliance with the 2015 Joint Comprehensive Plan of Action to Congress (JCPOA), He stated that Iran's behavior violated the spirit of the agreement. Trump did not take steps to repeal the JCPOA; but rather requested Congress to deliberate on reimposing sanctions.

Jerusalem 1. What better time to make an announcement about Jerusalem than right before the holidays? Trump broke with decades of diplomacy by saying the U.S. embassy would move from Tel Aviv to Jerusalem. This act officially recognized Jerusalem as the Capital of Israel. Until the new embassy is completed and reopened, the U.S. will remain in Tel Aviv, and the President will continue to sign a six-month waiver of congressional legislation. Trump clearly stated that the U.S. would not follow the practice of previous administrations that used the waiver to prevent taking any actions that would derail progress towards an Israeli-Palestinian settlement. Trump ignored requests from allies not to make any decisions that may be critical in a final resolution for the Middle East.

Trump's decision immediately brought worldwide criticism. Before his final announcement, he called leaders in the region, including Jordan's King Abdullah, Egypt's President Abdel Fattah al-Sisi, King Salman of Saudi Arabia, Israeli Prime Minister Benjamin Netanyahu, and Palestinian President Mahmoud Abbas. Kushner, who had been leading a diplomatic initiative for the Middle East, insisted his father-in-law's announcement would not disrupt his efforts.

Abbas warned Trump of the danger of such a decision to the Middle East peace efforts, in addition to the region's security and stability. Unilaterally recognizing Jerusalem as the Capital would violate international law, and the Palestinians would challenge the move at the U.N. Security Council.

King Abdullah, likewise, told Trump that this decision would have "dangerous repercussions on the stability and security of the region" and would obstruct U.S. efforts to resume Arab-Israeli peace talks.

King Salman told Trump: "Such a dangerous step is likely to inflame the passions of Muslims around the world due to the great status of Jerusalem and the al-Aqsa Mosque."

Even Pope Francis criticized the decision in his Christmas address. He called for a two-state solution to end the Israeli-Palestinian conflict. "Let us pray that the will to resume dialogue may prevail between the parties and that a negotiated solution can finally be reached, one that would allow the peaceful coexistence of two states within mutually agreed and internationally recognized borders to the city and the world. We see Jesus in the children of the Middle East who continue to suffer because of growing   tensions between Israelis and Palestinians."

<u>Jerusalem 2.</u> The U.S. vetoed a draft of the U.N. Security Council resolution that rejected Trump's decision to recognize Jerusalem as the Capital. The text, which was written by Egypt, affirmed that any decisions on the status of Jerusalem had "no legal effect, are null and void and must be rescinded." The 14 other members of the council voted in favor of the motion. Israeli Prime Minister Netanyahu thanked U.N. Representative Haley and Trump for the veto. Haley described the U.N. vote as an "insult" and warned it would not be forgotten. "It's one more example of the United Nations doing more harm than good in addressing the Israeli-Palestinian conflict."

Then the entire U.N. voted after Trump threatened to cut off financial aid to countries voting in favor. A total of 128 countries backed the resolution, 9 voted against, 35 abstained, and 21 did not vote. Haley once again came out strongly against those voting for the measure, threatening that she and Trump would be watching the ballot and taking names of those who did not vote in the their favor. She tweeted "At the U.N. we're always asked to do more & give more. So, when we make a decision, at the will   of the American where to locate OUR embassy, we don't expect those we've helped to target us. On Thurs there'll be a vote criticizing our choice. The U.S. will be taking names."

Haley then said, "We will no longer let the generosity of the American people be taken advantage of or remain unchecked." The U.S. negotiated a $285 million reduction of the U.N. budget for 2018 to 2019 compared to the budget for 2016 to 2017. This was $85 million more than the $200 million cut that was backed in October. The U.N. two-year budget has been roughly $5.5 billion,

Haley then held a party for the 64 representatives of nations who supported the U.S. and raged against the U.N. General Assembly members who condemned Trump's recognition of Jerusalem as Capital. Under the title, "A great evening of friends," Haley's Twitter page said, "It's easy for friends to be with you in the good times, but it's the friends who are with you during the challenging times that will never be forgotten. Thank you to the 64."

As a result, Palestinian President Abbas refused to meet Vice President Pence as previously planned. Part of the reason was that Pence was seen by the Palestinians as having been a key influence on Trump regarding the decision and appeared to have made little effect to repair the damage.

<u>Palestine.</u> Haley has not only supported Trump, she has been moving along on her own. She wanted to go one step further and cut off all funding to the U.N. agency that handles Palestinian refugees, in order to encourage the Palestinian leadership to re-enter peace talks with Israel. Secretary of State Tillerson overruled Haley and said the U.S. would give $50 million, a significant cut from the $125 million earlier determined.

<u>Worldwide.</u> Nations across the world were first laughing at Trump and then became increasingly worried about and angry at his comments and actions. During the laughter stage, Prime ministers from Denmark, Norway, Finland, Sweden and Iceland took photographs that made light of Trump's visit to Saudi

Arabia. When Trump was with Saudi Arabia's King Salman and Egypt's President Abdel Fattah el-Sisi, Trump placed his hands on a glowing globe of the Global Center for Combating Extremist Ideology. The Scandinavian leaders recreated the photograph with a soccer ball.

In January 2017, Dutch Jewish comedian, Greg Shapiro, introduced the "who wants to be Second if "America is First" viral campaign. This started a host of European countries vying for the title:

Russia. Trump blamed every person and every country throughout his campaign, to the day he was elected, and onward to 2018, which was very confusing and upsetting to Americans and government officials. If anything increased the idea of "collusion" ("There was no collusion!"), was Trump's support of Russia and Putin.
In January, he passed by a deadline to impose sanctions on individuals who do business with Russian military or intelligence entities. He did release a list from the Treasury Department of over 200 influential, wealthy Russians and senior government officials.
In addition to his ceaseless "no collusion" comments, Trump has been consistent on his positive comments or lack of negative comments about Russia. At the end of 2017, he stated as usual that Putin told him he didn't interfere in the U.S. elections."He said he didn't meddle. He said he didn't meddle. I asked him again. Every time he sees me, he said: 'I didn't do that.' And I believe -- I really believe -- that when he tells me that, he means it. You can only ask so many times.... He said he absolutely did not meddle in our election."

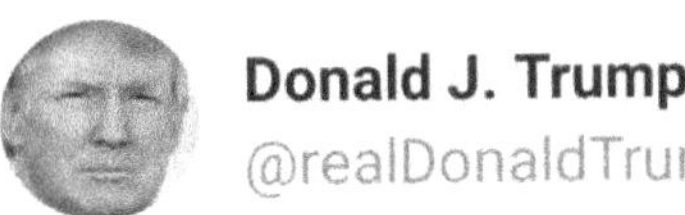

When will all the haters and fools out there realize that having a good relationship with Russia is a good thing, not a bad thing. There always playing politics - bad for our country. I want to solve North Korea, Syria, Ukraine, terrorism, and Russia can greatly help!

7:18 PM · 11 Nov 17 from Vietnam

(As this book was going to press, Putin was just reelected and Trump called him with congratulations ("despite his national security telling him DO NOT congratulate Putin"), Russia was being blamed for poisoning ex-spies in England, *Time* reported that "Russia Secretly Helped Venezuela Launch a Cryptocurrency to Evade U.S. Sanctions," and American sanctions on Russia continued to be mild.)

CHAPTER SEVEN: EASY COME, EASY GO

Saying there has was a great deal of turnover in the Trump Administration during 2017 is an understatement. In addition to not filling scores of positions, scores of people came, saw and did not conquer. Here is a list of them.

January 30: Sally Yates. The Acting Attorney General, a holdover from the Obama Administration, was dismissed after she refused to defend the first iteration of Trump's travel ban on citizens from seven Muslim-majority countries.

February 13: Michael Flynn. The National Security Adviser was mired in a controversy after news reports surfaced that he had misled officials, including Vice President Pence, about his communications with Russian Ambassador Kislyak. He resigned shortly afterward. He has since pled guilty of lying to the FBI.

March 11: Preet Bharara. Manhattan Federal Prosecutor Bharara was fired after he declined to willingly resign from his job, although Trump had previously said he supported him..

March 30: Katie Walsh. This Deputy Chief of Staff was fired after the House's first failure to repeal Obamacare.

April 9: K.T. McFarland. McFarland was appointed as Trump's Deputy National Security Adviser. She was supposed to be reassigned as ambassador to Singapore but withdrew her name.

May 5: Angella Reid. Chief Usher since 2011, she was the first woman to hold the position. Reid was fired for unclear reasons; it is unusual for chief ushers to be dismissed, they typically hold their positions for several years and over a number of administrations.

May 9: James Comey. The White House initially said Comey's firing was based on the Justice Department's recommendation over his handling of the Clinton email probe. Then Trump said he considered firing the FBI director even without that recommendation, and the Russia investigation was on his mind when making the decision.

May 9: John Thompson. This U.S. Census Bureau director served since 1975. There was no official reason given for his departure, but his exit came during a funding shortage. No replacement has been made, and the 2020 Census is looming.

May 18: Mike Dubke.. He handed in his resignation as White House Communications Director after three months on the job.

July 6: Walter Shaub. The Director of the Office of Government Ethics clashed repeatedly with the President before finally resigning.

July 21: Sean Spicer. The Press Secretary's chaotic tenure, marked by disagreements with the press, culminated with a firing/resignation when Trump hired Anthony Scaramucci as his new Communications Director.

July 25: Michael Short. The Senior Assistant Press Secretary, brought on by Priebus, resigned after Scaramucci said he would be fired for allegedly leaking to the press.

July 28: Reince Priebus. In his six-month tenure, marked by staff infighting and political revePresident win congressional legislation. He was followed by Kelly, with the hope that Trump could be reined in.

July 31: Anthony Scaramucci. The controversial Communications Director stepped down after 11 days on the job, the same day Kelly took over as Chief of Staff.

August. 18: Steve Bannon. An on-again, off-again confidant of Trump, Bannaon also left once Kelly arrived.

August 25: Sebastian Gorka. This controversial counterterrorism adviser, who awaited arrest in Hungary, left when Kelly revoked his security clearance.

August 30: Carl Ichan. He resigned as Special Advisor on Regulatory Reform amidst conflict-of-interest complaints.

September 1. Keith Schiller. This long-time aide and current Director of Oval Office Operations resigned.

September 29: Tom Price. The Health and Human Services Secretary resigned after revelations that he had piled up around $400,000 in private flights while traveling on official business.

November 24: Richard Cordray. He resigned from his post as the head of the Consumer Financial Protection Bureau , starting a disagreement between his former chief of staff and the White House over who would replace him. Before his resignation, Cordray promoted Chief of Staff Leandra English to the Deputy Director position, but the White House announced Mick Mulvaney, head of the Office of Management and Budget, as interim director.

Dec. 8: Dina Powell. Trump's Deputy National Security Adviser, who was a driving force behind the President's Middle East policy, resigned and returned to Goldman Sachs.

Dec. 13: Omarosa Manigault Newman. Political Aide in the Office of Public Liaison, she rose to notoriety when on "The Apprentice" with Trump. She voiced much concern over the White House and Trump after leaving.

Early 2018

January 5. Taylor Weyeneth. First appointed as White House Liaison to the Office of National Drug Control Policy and then promoted to Deputy Chief of Staff, he resigned after questions arose about qualifications on his resume.

January 18. Karl Higbe. Chief of External Affairs for the federal Corporation for National and Community Service resigned after racist, sexist, anti-Muslim and anti-LGBT radio comments from 2016 became known.

January 30. Andrew McCabe. He was expected to retire as FBI Deputy Director a month after this resignation.

January 31. Brenda Fitzgerald. Approved to be Director of the Centers for Disease Control and Prevention, she resigned after reports that she traded in tobacco stocks after assuming her position.

February 8: Rob Porter. This White House Staff Secretary resigned after allegations of physically abusing his two ex-wives.

February 9: Rachel Brand.. This Associate Attorney General held the third highest position in the Justice Department. Brand joined Walmart as Executive Vice President of Global Governance and Corporate Secretary.

February 11: David Sorenson. He resigned from his position as speechwriter after abuse allegations.

Rachel Maddow's list of resignations and firings.

(March 2018--McMaster is out and John Bolton is in, but can he get security clearance?)

CHAPTER EIGHT: TRUMP VS. THE MEDIA
(EXCEPT FOR FOX NEWS)

According to *The Atlantic,* "Trump is likely the most media-obsessed president in American history, and has long recognized and exploited its power to assist him, but he cleverly latched onto a decades-long conservative campaign to undermine the press." In the campaign, he regularly slammed the media for "fake news." During his Presidency, his comments have continued through Twitter each time he disagreed with the media's fact-based stories.

Even with positive news, Trump took potshots. *The Washington Examiner* reported that he accused the press of 'fake polls' designed to make it look like his State of the Union received widespread disapproval among viewers. "They came up with fake polls but the fake polls were even good," he said. A poll by CNN found that 48% of Americans watching the speech had a "very positive" impression.

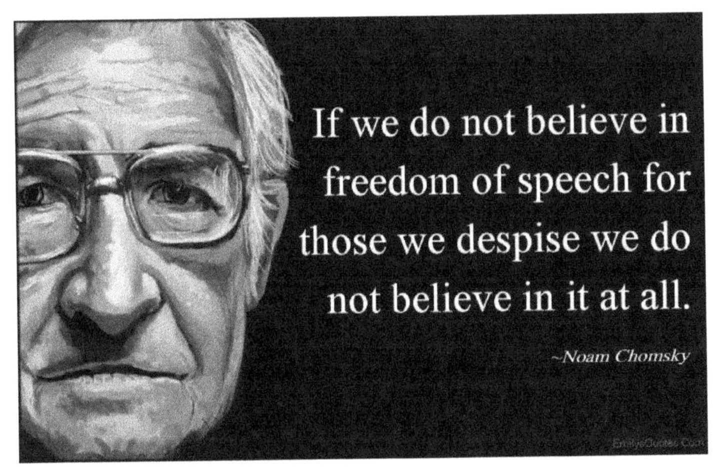

The Atlantic reported that "freedom of the press is in a beleaguered state." Not only have traditional economic models crumbled, but public support for the underlying venture is low. A January Gallup and Knight Foundation survey indicated that 8 of 10 Americans believe the news media is important in informing the public of current events and holding government officials responsible for their actions. However, just 33% of those surveyed have a favorable opinion of the news media, compared to 43% who view it unfavorably. Trust in mass media has declined since 1976, when 72% of Americans had much higher regard for them.

The inventor of the World Wide Web, Tim Berners-Lee, said that fake news was one of the three most upsetting Internet trends that has kept the Internet from truly "serving humanity." He said that this trend is spreading worldwide and that despots are using fake news as a weapon.

It is common knowledge that Trump changed his views on most things from one day to the next, depending on a number of factors. However, he began changing his mind from one minute to the next, while negating his own Republican Congress. He would see a Fox TV news commentary and became confused about the facts. Republicans were voting on a Foreign Intelligence Surveillance Act (FISA), which lets agencies collect information on foreign targets abroad. Despite his administration's support for FISA's renewal, Trump tweeted, "This is the act that may have been used, with the help of the discredited and phony Dossier, to so badly surveil and abuse the Trump Campaign by the previous administration and others?"

Then Trump received a call to let him know that he was confused and should be in favor of the renewal. He posted a follow-up tweet clarifying that he had sought changes to the law and was voicing support for the surveillance program. "With that being said, I have personally directed the fix to the unmasking process since taking office and today's vote is about foreign surveillance of foreign bad guys on foreign land. We need it! Get smart!".

Who Knows What Is True and What Is False?

FROM JANUARY 2017 TO JANUARY 2018, TRUMP TOLD AT LEAST 2,000 FALSE OR MISLEADING CLAIMS, said *The Washington Post*. That works out to approximately five to six incorrect comments a day. In fact, the longer he is President, the more lies he his telling.

Then, There Is The Problem With White House Accuracy

Maybe it is because the Trump Administration does not have a large enough staff. Or, perhaps the people working for Trump are not good proofreaders. Or maybe, they are just not knowledgeable. The number of mistakes in transcriptions, schedules, and press releases has clearly demonstrated the quality of the administrative staff. They include:

A press statement about the Middle East sought to promote "**the possibility of lasting peach."**

A White House media list of global terror attacks contained such words as "**Attaker,"** **"San Bernadino" and "Denmakr."**

British Prime Minister Theresa May's name was misspelled several times, including as **"Teresa May,"** or the name of a porn star.

A message to schools receiving the President's Education Award spelled "success" as **"succuess**." Some errors, such as this one, were caught and changed, and others, such as **"Normay"** instead of "Norway," stayed the same. There was also the **State of the Uniom** tickets.

The acorn does not fall far away from the tree, since Trump's tweets include misspellings, such as "heel" for "heal." :Many times, Trump does not know what is right versus what is wrong. His supporters say that he is not "stupid" but "ignorant." Trump watches a lot of TV, which everyone knows by his immediate response to news shows. However, he does not read books or even long articles. "I never have," he proudly told a reporter. "I'm always busy doing a lot." As President, Trump's intelligence briefings (when/if he has them) have been very brief and simple and filled with maps and pictures, because he cannot be bothered to read a lot of words. If his staff want him to read the briefs, they are sure to put his name in frequently.
The first major typo on a Trump tweet read, "Despite the constant negative press covfefe ('coverage.')." Rumors went around that something had happened to the President and did not know right from wrong.
Here are some other Trump typos. How hard is it to use spell check or proof what is written?:

"Karen **Handle's** opponent in #GA06 can't even vote in the district he wants to represent."

"With all of the illegal acts that took place in the Clinton campaign & Obama Administration, there was never a special **councel** appointed!".

"Ask Sally Yates, under oath, if she knows how classified information got into the newspapers soon after she explained it to W.H. **Council**.".

"Buy American & hire American are the **principals** at the core of my agenda, which is: JOBS, JOBS, JOBS! Thank you @exxonmobil."

"Terrible! Just found out that Obama had my '**wires tapped**' in Trump Tower just before the victory. Nothing found. This is McCarthyism!

Trump was **honered** to be President.

"Wow, every poll said I won the debate last night. Great **honer**!" he tweeted and deleted February 26, 2016.

"China steals United States Navy research drone in international waters - rips it out of water and takes it to China in **unpresidented** act."

If Russia, or some other entity, was hacking, why did the White House **waite** so long to act? Why did they only complain after Hillary lost?"

"Reports by @CNN that I will be working on The Apprentice during my Presidency, even part time, are **rediculous** & untrue - FAKE NEWS!"

"Saturday's attacks show that failed Obama/Hillary Clinton **polices** won't keep us safe! I will Make America Safe Again!"

"Looks to me like the Bernie people will fight. If not, **there** blood, sweat and tears was a total **waist** of time. Kaine stands for opposite!"

"The weekend in Texas and Arizona **wss** fantastic. I raised a lot of money for the Republican National Committee @Reince."

Hillary has bad **judgement!**"

"I will be campaigning in Indiana all day. Things are looking great, and the support of Bobby **Night** has been so amazing. Today will be fun!"

"@AndreaTantaros-You are a true journalistic **profesional.** I so agree with what you say. Keep up the great work!"

"These politicians like Cruz and Graham, who have watched ISIS and many other problems **develope** for years, do nothing to make thing better!,"

"The people of South Carolina are embarrassed by Nikki **Hailey**!"

"All of the phony T.V. commercials against me are bought and payed for by SPECIAL INTEREST GROUPS, the bandits that tell your **pols** what to do."

"Lying Ted Cruz and **leightweight chocker** Marco Rubio teamed up last night in a last ditch effort to stop our great movement. They failed!"

"Ted Cruz is totally unelectable, if he even gets to run (born in Canada). Will **loose** big to Hillary. Polls show I beat Hillary easily! WIN!"

"The dying @NRO National Review has totally given up the fight against **Barrack** Obama. They have been losing for years. I will beat Hillary!"

Other White House Errors Included:

Nambia. When Trump spoke to African leaders at the U.N., he twice referenced the country "Nambia." For example, he said, "Nambia's health system is increasingly self-sufficient." Did Trump invent a new nation or combine two existing ones--Zambia and Namibia?

F-52 Fighters..Trump announced that the first of "F-52 and F-35" fighter jets had been delivered to Norway -- proudly touting the "$10 billion" sale of military equipment to the NATO ally during a news conference with the Norwegian prime minister. The F-52 fighter jet has never existed, except in video games. He was referring to the F-35, being purchased by Japan, Israel, the United Kingdom, Italy, Norway, Belgium, Denmark and Turkey.

Germany1. When Trump talked trade deals with Germany, he said, "Hopefully we can even it out. We don't want victory, we want fairness. All I want is fairness." Merkel looked confused: Germany has no trade deal with the U.S.

Germany2 Trump stated that Germany owed "vast sums" to the U.S. for NATO. Not true. No NATO member has ever paid the U.S. for NATO.

Hezbollah.. Trump said, "Lebanon is on the front lines in the fight against ISIS, Al Qaeda, and Hezbollah." For the past quarter century, Hezbollah has been part of the Lebanese government with seats in parliament and cabinet posts. Lebanon's Christian President Michel Aoun has been allied with Hezbollah for a decade. While Trump was speaking, Hezbollah's militia and the Lebanese Army were fighting ISIS and an Al Qaeda affiliate occupying a part of eastern Lebanon along its border with Syria. They won.

Korea.. Trump claimed that Korea "actually used to be part of China."

France. When visiting France, Trump confused Emperor Napoleon Bonaparte with Napoleon III, who was France's first popularly elected president, oversaw the design of modern Paris and was the longest serving head of state since the French Revolution.

Kurdistan.. In an interview with conservative radio host Hugh Hewitt, Trump appeared to combine the Kurdish people with the Iranian Revolutionary Guard's overseas force, as well as confuse the names and leaders of various Islamist extremist groups. "Well, that is a gotcha question, though," Trump protested to Hewitt when asked whether he was familiar with the leaders of Hamas, Hezbollah and ISIS. "I mean, you know, when you're asking me about who's running this, this this, that's not, that is not, I will be so good at the military, your head will spin."

Christian Religions..Trump met with pastors of two major Presbyterian churches in New York. "I did very, very well with evangelicals in the polls," he told them. When the pastors answered that they weren't evangelicals, he demanded to know, "What are you then?" They told him they were mainline Presbyterians. "But you're all Christians?" he asked. Yes, they had to assure him, Presbyterians are Christians. Trump, in fact, is Presbyterian.

New Words.. Trump believed he coined the word "fake news." Similarly, he asked *Economist* editors if they had heard of the phrase "priming the pump." Yes, they assured him, they had. "I haven't heard it," Trump continued. "I mean, I just … I came up with it a couple of days ago, and I thought it was good." The phrase has been used since the 1930s, or before.

Andrew Jackson.. The President said that President Andrew Jackson, with whom he feels aligned, had strong thoughts about the Civil War--even though Jackson died 16 years before the war occurred. "He was really angry that -- he saw what was happening with regard to the Civil War. He said, 'There's no reason for this.'" When Trump heard about his error, he made the correction on Twitter: "President Jackson, who died 16 years before the Civil War started, saw it coming and was angry. Would never let it happen."

Abraham Lincoln.. Most people do not know that Lincoln was a Republican, Trump said in a tweet. "Great President!" At one of his speeches, he added, "Republicans need to spread the word that Lincoln was a Republican," not aware that the GOP is commonly referred to as the "Party of Lincoln." "Let's take an ad, let's use one of those PACs," he said.

Frederick Douglass.. At a February event commemorating Black History Month, Trump expounded on the virtues of Frederick Douglass, the Civil War-era abolitionist, as if he were still alive. "Frederick Douglass is an example of somebody who's done an amazing job and is getting recognized more and more, I notice," he said.

American Healthcare.. During the crafting of the House bill to partially repeal and replace Obama's Affordable Care Act, Trump explained that he only just learned that making one change in the healthcare system has multiple effects in other areas. "Nobody knew healthcare could be so complicated," he said.

U.S. Military..Trump's lack of understanding about the U.S. military has even upset the Republicans. During a veterans' town hall, he proposed setting up a military court system that already exists, wrongly suggested military generals are political appointees who change over when a new president arrives, and continued to insist that America should have "taken the oil" after leaving Iraq — an action that would have violated the Geneva Convention.

Richard Nixon.. In an interview with *The Washington Post's* Bob Woodward, who broke the Watergate story leading to President Nixon's impeachment, Trump implied that Nixon failed because of his personality. Woodward asked Trump why he thought Lincoln succeeded and Nixon did not. Trump blamed Nixon's temperament. "Nixon failed, I think to a certain extent, because of his personality. It was just that personality. Very severe, very exclusive. In other words, people couldn't come in. And people didn't like him. I mean, people didn't like him."

North Korea. When interviewed on Fox & Friends, Trump mixed up current leader Kim Jong Un with his predecessor and father Kim Jong II. "They've been talking with this gentleman for a long time," Trump said of America and North Korea.

The Holocaust.. On Holocaust Remembrance Day, the White House acknowledged "the victims, survivors, heroes" of the Holocaust, but did not specifically recognize the six million Jews who died. Many Americans took this omission as an act of anti-Semitism.

Some False/Fake Trump Comments

"More people watched the (Trump) inauguration than ever before."

"We're having tremendous plans coming out now — health care plans — at a fraction of the cost that are much better than Obamacare."

"I never said Russia did not meddle in our election."

"Hillary Clinton won the popular vote because of fraud."

"Michael Flynn didn't do 'anything wrong."

"Obama bugged Trump Tower."

"Charlottesville Counterprotesters lacked a permit."

"America pays the most taxes."

"Tax reform will cost me a fortune."

"I will be showing my income tax forms in two weeks."

"The Kate Steinle killer came back and back over the weakly protected Obama border, always committing crimes and being violent, and yet this info was not used in court. His exoneration is a complete travesty of justice. BUILD THE WALL!"

"As a candidate, I pledge to fight for American jobs. I think it's possibly the number-one reason I got elected. And I think we've done a lot better, at this point, than anybody ever even thought possible. Think of that, two million jobs since the election--two million more jobs in this country since the election. Nobody expected that. Nobody expected that."

"In all fairness, the stock market was going this way (Trump drawing flat line with hand)."

"Me, it's not so--I have some very wealthy friends--not so happy with me. But that's okay. You know, I keep hearing Schumer. 'This is for the wealthy.' Well, if it is, my friends don't know about it." (about tax reform)

"Since the first day I took office, all you hear is the phony Democrat excuse for losing the election. Russia, Russia, Russia. Despite this, I have the economy booming and have possibly done more than any 10-month President make America great again."

"The last thing we need in Alabama and the U.S. Senate is a Schumer/Pelosi puppet who is weak on crime, weak on border, bad for our military and our great vets, bad for our 2nd Amendment and wants to raise taxes to the sky. Jones would be a disaster."

"I got a call from the head of the Boy Scouts saying it was the greatest speech that was ever made to them." (after the Boy Scout Jamboree)

"Mexico's President Enrique Penanieto paid me the 'ultimate compliment' by calling and telling me that 'their southern border, very few people are coming because they know they're not going to get through our border."

"I'm a very big person when it comes to the environment. I have received awards on the environment."

The New York Times conducted a thorough accounting of all of Trump's lies in 2017. Here is breakdown of these falsehoods.

A year-end review of untrue claims from FactCheck.org found Trump dominating the list with remarks on everything from his inauguration to the Russia investigation to his own tax bill. Of PolitiFact's 483 fact checking on Trump, 69% were rated "mostly false," "false," or "pants on fire." His claims on Russian meddling were the "lie of the year."

A year-end Quinnipiac poll reported that 62% of voters don't think Trump was honest. While only 34% believe he was. While Republicans remained trusting with 75% believing he was honest, more than two-thirds of independents did not agree, and a very high 93% of Democrats thought he was dishonest, compared to 52% of voters who thought the same after the November election--a ten-point decline over 2017-2018.

FIRST 40 DAYS OF TRUMP ADMINISTRATION

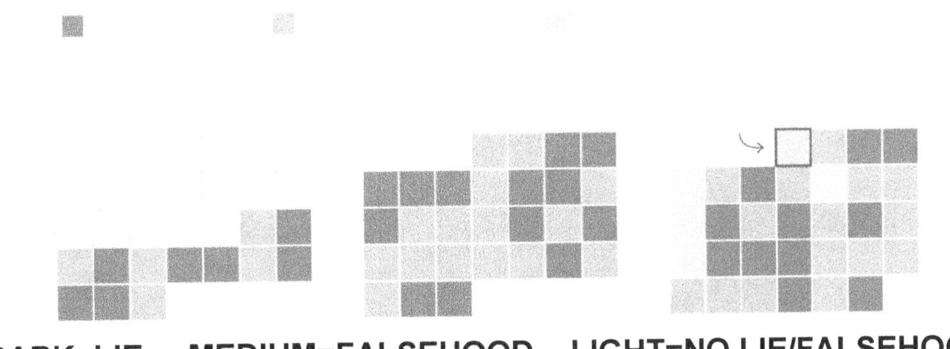

DARK=LIE   MEDIUM=FALSEHOOD   LIGHT=NO LIE/FALSEHOOD

The New York Times explained that Trump told a public lie on at least 20 of his 40 days in office. However, based on misleading statements (exaggerations, e.g.), he achieved "something remarkable." He said something untrue, in public, every day for the first 40 days of his Presidency. This streak did not end until March 1, 2017.

The Gaslighting of Sarah Huckabee Sanders

Being the spokesperson for the President of the U.S. has never been an easy position--particularly when the President is known for lies and deception. Sarah Huckabee Sanders has been an exceptional White House Press Secretary. Only a couple of times has she actually shown any anger toward the media; in fact, from time to time she has made her own jokes about the proceedings. She has been calm, cool and unflappable, despite the stress of having to speak for Trump. She has truly deserved an award for being the best at her job. Politifact pointed out a number of her falsehoods over 2017 including:

Diversity visa immigrants are not vetted.
— *PolitiFact National on Thursday, November 2nd, 2017*

"The president in no way, form or fashion has ever promoted or encouraged violence."
— *PolitiFact National on Wednesday, July 5th, 2017*

"Everybody acts like President Trump is the one that came up with this idea. ... There are multiple news outlets that have reported" former President Barack Obama ordered wiretapping on Trump.
— *PolitiFact National on Sunday, March 5th, 2017*

The term "gaslighting" has now been associated with Sanders. Wikipedia defines gaslighting: as "a form of manipulation that seeks to sow seeds of doubt…in members of a targeted group, hoping to make them question their own memory, perception, and sanity. Using persistent denial, misdirection, contradiction, and lying, it attempts to destabilize the target and delegitimize the target's belief." In other words, it goes beyond lying and becomes a form of manipulation.

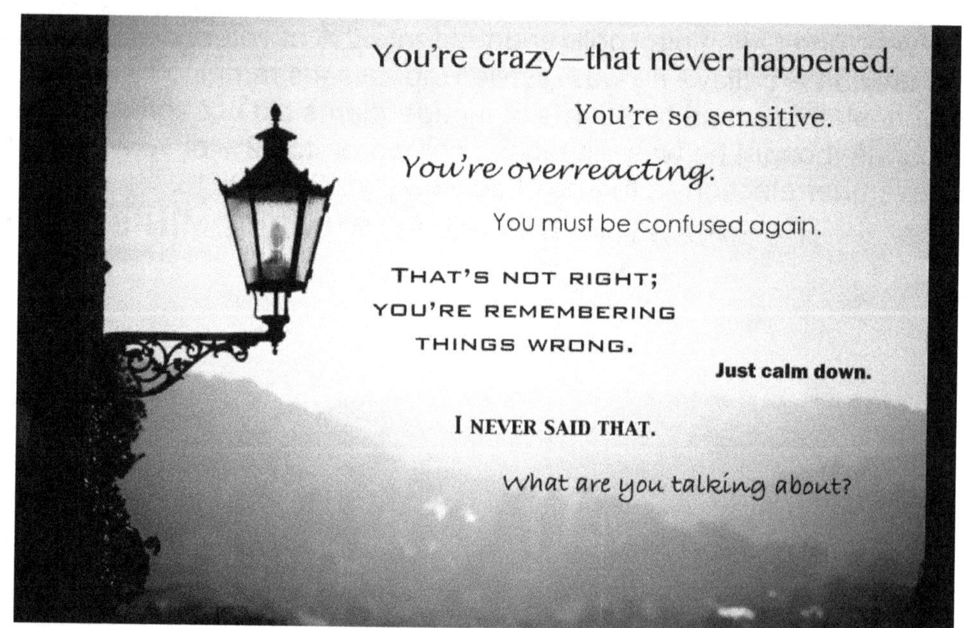

CHAPTER NINE: BULLY FOR YOU, BULLY!

Trump called people names throughout his campaign, which did not end. with his Presidency whenever he was angry with someone. However, those who called Trump names, particularly the Republicans, during the election stopped doing so once he was President.

Some of Trump Nicknames for his Foes

Little Adam Schiff
Little Rocket Man
Sloppy Steve
Pocahontas
Dicky Durbin
Mr. Magoo
Sneaky Dianne Feinstein
Jeff Flakey
Al Frankenstien
Liddle' Bob Corker
Wacky Congresswoman Wilson
Crooked Hillary
Crying Chuck
Leakin' James Comey
Puppet Jones
The Amazon *Washington Post*
The Failing *New York Times*

They Love You, They Love You Not

<u>Senator Marco Rubio.</u> Trump and Rubio used words to fight each other throughout the entire election. Most of these slams had to do with each other's physical attributes, such as sweating and meltdowns, short height and small hands, large ears and orange face. They also threw barbs about topics such as their intelligence, with Trump saying that Rubio could not get into the Wharton School at University of Pennsylvania and Rubio saying that Trump continually misspelled words.

Yet, in 2017, the two bonded over foreign affairs with Venezuela and Cuba. Rubio was pleased that Trump revamped Obama's Cuba policies. When making a speech in Miami after Trump was elected, Rubio recalled a conversation between the two of them after the election: "One of the first things he said to me is, 'What are we going to do to help the Cuban people?'"

Rubio added: "The cooperation, the hard work, the commitment that this White House and President Trump has shown to this cause, I believe has no precedent, certainly in the modern history of this great cause."

When Trump took the stage at this Florida event, he repaid the praise: "I want to express our deep gratitude to a man who has really become a friend of mine, and I want to tell you, he's one tough competitor, Sen. Marco Rubio, great guy," Trump said. "He is tough. Man. He is tough, and he is good, and he loves you."

Senator Ted Cruz: During the election, Cruz and Trump boxed it out with unfriendly names, such as "Lyin' Ted," and Trump even made fun of Cruz' wife's look. Cruz called Trump a "pathological liar," "utterly amoral," "a narcissist at a level I don't think this country's ever seen" and "a serial philanderer." Later, when Trump received the endorsement, Cruz backed him on Facebook.

Yet, Cruz, his wife and children visited Trump in the White House for dinner. "It was a social evening," Cruz told reporters. "We had a very nice evening with the President and first lady, with Heidi and the girls. Catherine was most excited to bring Joe with her, the stuffed giraffe from her kindergarten class who every student takes home for a few days. And so Joe had a chance to have dinner with the president, which was a fun thing."

Senator Lindsey Graham. The Senator had backed Jeb Bush for President and said Trump was a "kook," "crazy," and "unfit for office." He slammed Trump for not being a real Republican, and said he was not suitable for the Presidency. "I'm a Republican, and he's not. He's not a conservative Republican, he's an opportunist. He's not fit to be President of the United States." Although Graham came out against Trump from time to time, agreeing on the issues kept them close together. According to "FiveThirtyEight," the following was true for January 2017 to February 2018 for Graham and Trump.

Trump score	**Trump margin**	**Predicted score**	**Trump plus-minus**
How often Graham voted in line with Trump's position: 88.1%	Trump's share of the vote in the 2016 election in South Carolina minus Clinton's: 14.3%	How often Graham was expected to support Trump based on Trump's 2016 margin: 79.2%	Difference between Graham's actual and predicted Trump-support scores: +9.0

By the end of 2017, Graham and Trump were playing golf together, and Graham in an interview with *Politico* insisted that Trump was "growing into the job" and was far different from the person he routinely railed against over the past two years. "Part of it's just getting to know each other better," Graham said, adding, "I do better in South Carolina when I'm seen as helping him, 'cause he's popular. When I'm helping him, he's seen as being able to reach out to an old critic. One thing he likes, I think, about me, is I don't quit."

It was not only Presidential contenders who changed their tune once Trump had won the election. His White House team and cabinet soon learn that Trump loves to hear positive comments about himself. Several times over the year, At a couple of meetings, these men and women told Trump what they thought about working with Trump.

Vice President Pence. "It is just the greatest privilege of my life is to serve as the -- as Vice President to the President who's keeping his word to the American people and assembling a team that's bringing real change, real prosperity, real strength back to our nation," buttered-up Pence.

Chief of Staff Priebus.. Priebus (no longer around) spoke up to thank Trump "for the opportunity and blessing that you've given us to serve your agenda and the American people."

Defense Secretary Mattis. "Mr. President, it's an honor to represent the men and women of the Department of Defense. And we are grateful for the sacrifices our people are making in order to strengthen our military so our diplomats always negotiate from a position of strength. Thank you," said Mattis.

Attorney General Sessions.. "It's an honor to be able to serve you," said Sessions (does he still feel the same way after being berated by Trump?).

Homeland Security Secretary Kelly. "In the five months that I've been at the job, we have gone a long way to facilitate the -- improve the legal movement of people and commerce across our borders, yet at the same time, we have gone a long way to safeguarding our borders, particularly the southern border, working with all of our partners to the south," noted Kelly in his previous position..

U.S Trade Representative Lighthizer. "First of all, I apologize for being late to work. I got bogged down in that swamp that you've been trying to drain," said Lighthizer.

Energy Secretary Perry.. "My hat is off to you," said Energy Secretary Perry, referring to how pleased everyone was that Trump pulled out of the climate change agreement."

Secretary of State Tillerson.. Thank you for the honor to serve the country. It's a great privilege you've given me," claimed Tillerson, who supposedly later called Trump "a f__ing moron,"

Secretary of the Interior Zinke. "Mr. President, as your SEAL on your staff ... it's an honor to be   your steward of our public lands and the generator of energy dominance. I am deeply honored," said the Secretary of the Interior, who is cutting these public lands.

Education Secretary. "It's a privilege to serve, to serve the students of this country, and to work to ensure that every child has an equal opportunity to get a great education, and therefore a great future," noted DeVos, who does not understand that money stands for equal opportunity.

Director of National Intelligence Coats. It's a joy to be working with the people that I have inherited, and we are going to provide -- continue to provide you with the very best intelligence we can, so you can formulate policies to deal with these issues," agreed Coats.

Commerce Secretary Ross. "Mr. President, thank you for the opportunity to help fix the trade deficit and other things. The other countries are gradually getting used to the (inaudible) the free rides are somewhat over with. They're not happy with this, but I think (inaudible) growing recognition that (inaudible) have a chance to help you live up to your campaign promises," explained Ross, who also does not understand what having or not having money means.

Housing and Urban Development Secretary Carson. "Mr.President, it's been a great honor to -- to work with you. Thank you for your strong support of HUD and for all the others around this table that I've worked with," mumbled Carson.

U.N. Ambassador Haley. "It's a new day at the United Nations. You know, we now have a very strong voice. People know what the United States is for, they know what we're against, and they see us leading across the board. And so, I think the international community knows we're back," said Haley.

Office of Management and Budget Director Mulvaney "Thanks for the kind words about the budget. You're absolutely right: We are going to be able to take care of the people who really need it. And at the same time, with your direction, we were able to also focus on the forgotten man and woman who are the folks who are paying those taxes," Mulvaney said.

Labor Secretary Acosta.. "I am privileged to be here. Deeply honored, and I want to thank you for being -- your commitment to the American workers," extolled Acosta..

Veteran Affairs Secretary Shulkin. "Mr. President, thank you for your support and commitment to honoring our responsibility to America's veterans. I know that this is personally very important to you," stated Shulkin, who does care about the veterans.

Secretary of the Treasury Mnuchin. "It was a great honor traveling with you around the country for the last year and an even greater honor to be here serving on your Cabinet," said Mnuchin.

Transportation Secretary Chao.. "Mr. President, last week was a great (inaudible). It was infrastructure week. Thank you so much for coming over to the Department of Transportation. Hundreds and hundreds of people were just so thrilled, hanging out, watching (inaudible) ceremony, " amazingly said Chao, despite infrastructure not being mentioned for the rest of the year.

CIA Director Mike Pompeo.. "Mr. President, it's an honor to serve as your CIA director. It's an incredible privilege to lead the men and women who are providing intelligence so that we can do the national security mission. And in the finest traditions of the CIA, I'm not going to share a d*mn thing in front of the media," Pompeo promised, as the White House continued and still continues to leak.

<u>Agriculture Secretary Purdue</u>."I want to congratulate you on the men and women you've placed around this table. ... This is the team you've assembled that's working hand in glove with -- for the men and women of America, and I want to -- I want to thank you for that. These are -- are great team members and we're on your team," praised Purdue. And, good for him, who praised Trump by praising everyone else.

<u>Secretary of Health and Human Services Price.</u> "Mr. President, what an incredible honor it is to lead the Department of Health and Human Services at this pivotal time under your leadership. I can't thank you enough for the privileges you've given me and the leadership that you've shown. It seems like there's an international flair to the messages that are being delivered. I had the opportunity to represent the United States at the G-20 Health Summit in Berlin and at the World Health Assembly in Geneva. And I can't tell you how excited and enthusiastic folks are about the United States leadership as it relates to global health security," said now-ousted Price, who, unfortunately, wanted too many privileges.

<u>Speaker of the Senate</u> <u>McConell.</u> After the tax bill was passed, McConnell praised Trump for all he had done during the year, using all the right words like "you hold the record."
"This has been a year of extraordinary accomplishment for the Trump administration. We've cemented the Supreme Court to the right of center for a generation. Mr. President, thanks to your nominees we put 12 circuit court judges in place — the most since the circuit court system was established in 1891. You hold the record."

<u>Speaker of the House Ryan.</u> How to follow up on this? Ryan did: "Something this big, something this generational, something this profound could not have been done without exquisite presidential leadership. Mr. President, thank you for getting us over the finish line; thank you for getting us where we are."

<u>Vice President Pence.</u> Then, Pence crooned, "Thank you Mr. President. Thank you for your leadership. Thank you for your boundless faith in the American people, and thank you for keeping your promise to see this Congress deliver the largest tax cut in American history before Christmas of this year." If that wasn't enough, he added. "You, will make America great again."

<u>Senator Orrin Hatch.</u> If that was not enough... "You're living up to everything I thought you would," said Hatch. "You're one heck of a leader. Look at all the things that he's been able to get done, by sheer will in many ways. "I just hope that we all get behind him every way we can. This presidency could be the greatest presidency we have seen not only in generations but maybe ever."

<u>Trump Supports Other Trumps.</u> Of all people to back...The President threw his full support behind Republican Roy Moore in the Alabama Senate race. Eight women came forward with accusations of sexual misconduct against Moore. Three of the women alleged that he had sexually assaulted them. Moore was 31 with an alleged incident with a then-16-year-old and 32 with an alleged incident with the then-14-year-old.. The six other women recalled Moore pursuing romantic relationships or engaging in inappropriate or unwanted behavior with them, while they were between the ages of 16 and 22. The age of consent in Alabama is 16.

<u>Trump Pardons Other Trumps</u>. He made his first Presidential pardon of Sheriff Joe Arpaio way before his predecessors. "Throughout his time as Sheriff, Arpaio continued his life's work of protecting the public from the scourges of crime and illegal immigration," the White House said in a statement. "Sheriff Joe Arpaio is now 85 years old, and after more than 50 years of honorable service to our Nation, he is [a] worthy candidate for a Presidential pardon."

Arpaio ranked among the most controversial law-enforcement officials in American history. Phoenix-area voters elected him six times to lead the Maricopa County Sheriff's Department in Arizona. In many ways, his administrative oversight was very similar to Trump's. Arpaio's harsh treatment of undocumented immigrants and criminal suspects led to multiple civil-rights lawsuits. He claimed former Obama's birth certificate was a forgery even after Trump himself had publicly agreed that And he shared Trump's disdain for the federal judiciary, frequently castigating the judges who oversaw lawsuits against him. Arpaio was condemned by many people because of his racial bias. A 2011 Justice Department report concluded that he engaged in "unconstitutional policing" by frequently targeting Latinos for racial profiling. In response to a lawsuit, a federal judge ordered Arpaio to stop detaining and harassing residents of largely Latino neighborhoods. He ignored the order and continued to perform sweeps, claiming they were lawful. In 2015, the judge charged him with civil and criminal contempt and a misdemeanor offense. A federal court found him guilty. Trump's pardon came before Arpaio fulfilled his sentence of a maximum of six months in prison.

<u>Trump and "Me-Too"</u> At least 15 women have publicly accused Trump of sexual harassment and assault including being groped, fondled and forcibly kissed. "This was serial misconduct and perversion on the part of Mr. Trump. Unfortunately, this behavior isn't rare in our society, and people of all backgrounds can be victims. The only reason I am here today is that this offender is now the President of our country," said Rachel Crooks, who accused Trump of kissing her on the mouth without her consent in 2005. Samantha Holvey, the former Miss North Carolina, accused Trump of inspecting beauty pageant contestants in their dressing room, and Jessica Leeds, accused him of grabbing her chest and attempting to move his hand up her skirt on an airplane flight.

The White House responded that these allegations occurred long before he was President and Trump had "addressed these accusations directly and denied all of these allegations."

CHAPTER TEN: MENTALLY FIT FOR WHAT?

Even before Trump won the election, and surely after a couple of months in office, psychiatrists were already warning Americans that he was mentally ill. His narcissism, a disorder detailed in The *Diagnostic and Statistical Manual of Mental Disorders* by the American Psychiatric Association, is a pathology that makes him incapable of running a country--particularly a democracy.

Trump leads his life under a world of delusions, or fixed false beliefs that are resistant to truth or actual fact. For example, regardless of how many times one tells Trump that fewer people came to his inauguration than Obama's, he will not believe it. He will look for conspiracy theories that make his falsehoods true so that he is not seen to be wrong. He cannot personally tolerate being wrong.

In Michael Wolff's book *Fire and Fury,* Trump is described as a child by everyone working in the White House. Yet, Trump's follow-up tweet said how he was a "genius." Who else could be as successful as he has been? he questioned. From watching Fox TV, he knows "more about ISIS than the generals" and believes that among all human beings on the planet, "I alone can fix it." In addition, his continual lies, lack of concern about others' rights and treatment of women as well as his complete denial of any wrong, have clearly proven Trump's illness.

Narcissistic Personality Disorder (inflated sense of self-importance; an extreme preoccupation with one's self)

The diagnosis of narcissism was first defined in 1964 as a severe mental sickness representing "the quintessence of evil" by psychoanalyst and holocaust survivor Erich Fromm. Otto Kernberg, a psychoanalyst who specialized in borderline personalities, explained that malignant narcissism had four components: narcissism, paranoia, antisocial personality and sadism. Trump's actions this past year have demonstrated all four of these traits. He said he knows more than anyone else. Everyone believes him. He is always right: This narcissism makes him have a grandiose sense of self-importance, regardless of what he has achieved or not.

Trump's father and grandfather acted similarly, and Trump was a bully at a very young age. His success in business and then in entertainment enhanced this bravado. Whenever he has been demeaned, he has come out fighting. When he has been praised, he manically attempts to do more. In both cases, his behavior has deteriorated. In an article article, "1988: the Year Donald Lost his Mind," Michael Kruse wrote, "His response to his surging celebrity" after the publication of *The Art of The Deal* "was a series of manic, ill-advised ventures" that led to bankruptcy and divorce.

Impulsivity is another trait. Trump's behavior with North Korea was not only embarrassing but frightening, especially when he touted his bigger nuclear button. *Newsweek* painted this scenario: "One nightmare scenario goes like this: Donald Trump emerges from his White House bedroom in the middle of the night, cell phone in hand, enraged by the latest taunt from North Korea's Kim Jong Un. He spots the military aide sitting in the corridor with a black valise in his lap. It's called the nuclear football. 'I'm gonna take care of this son of a bitch once and for all," Trump growls. "Big-time. Gimme the codes.'" Only three days after Trump saw photos of gassed Syrian children, he launched 59 Tomahawk missiles at the Assad regime.

In *Fire and Fury*, Wolff also wrote about the concerns among top White House aides over Trump's psychological fitness for the presidency. The staff frequently mention Trump's "repetitions," which are common when someone is under a great deal of stress. "It used to be inside of 30 minutes he'd repeat, word-for-word and expression-for-expression, the same three stories – now it was within 10 minutes. Indeed, many of his tweets were the product of his repetitions – he just couldn't stop saying something."

Yale psychiatrist Bandy X. Lee met with a dozen people in Congress about Trump's worrisome mental health state. "Lawmakers were saying they have been very concerned about this, the President's dangerousness, the dangers that his mental instability poses on the nation," Lee said. "They know the concern is universal among Democrats, but it really depends on Republicans, they said. Some knew of Republicans that were concerned, maybe equally concerned, but whether they would act on those concerns was their worry."

When asked if she feared confrontation with North Korea, Lee said, "Yes, but that is not the only danger we're facing. There's everything in between: provoking our allies and alienating them, instigating civil conflict, and laying a foundation for a violent culture that could give way to epidemics of violence — not to mention poke a beehive in the Middle East by declaring Jerusalem as Israel's capital. All of these actions are consistent with the pathological pattern he has already shown of resorting to violence the more he feels threatened.

In the book, *The Dangerous Case of Donald Trump: 27 Psychiatrists and Mental Health Experts Assess a President*, Lee commented: "First, let me say, I speak for myself and not for my university. The book predicts danger and dangerousness. We have already seen this unfold. Basically, in "The Dangerous Case of Donald Trump" we were stating that past violence predicts future violence. Trump has shown verbal aggressiveness. He has boasted about sexual assault. He has invited violence at his rallies. He has shown an attraction to violence as a powerful weapon. He had not yet taunted a hostile nuclear power at that point. But in the book we actually predicted that devastating wars and even a nuclear holocaust were not impossibilities.

"Now, it is even clearer that the danger we predicted about Donald Trump has happened on many levels. There has been an unprecedented spike in hate crimes since the day after his election. This trend has not yet abated. There has been an escalation in gun deaths since Trump's campaign. There are also reports documenting how a large proportion of extremist violence and domestic terrorism is coming from white supremacists.

"The other dangers, of course, are his psychological instability. This includes Trump's impulsivity, recklessness, paranoid reactions, loose grip on reality, rage, lack of empathy, and the constant need to project and abuse power. His speech patterns have also changed. All these things have gotten worse over time. These all have profound ramifications for a person in his position of authority and power.":

The Republicans Are Blind

Many could see Trump's erratic behavior and heard about him "losing it and" yelling at everyone as well as the chaos in the White House. Over the year, more and more people started leaving their jobs either through resignations or firings. Most Republicans did not say anything about this behavior. Instead, they made excuses such as "he's learning," or "we never expected him to be like anyone else." As time went on, a few Republicans began to make comments, but these had nothing to lose; they decided not to run for office again.

Senator Bob Corker warned that the President's irresponsibility could lead the U.S. to World War III. Corker added that "the vast majority" of his fellow Republican Senators know "what we're dealing with here." They feel the same about Trump's childlike temperament. However, they will talk to each other quietly but not make any public comments. Unfortunately, they are more worried about their own future than that of the country. Speaker Ryan and Majority Leader McConnell did not want to rock the boat, since they were more concerned about avoiding conflict and getting bills passed.

Trump started a tweet war with Kim Jong-un from North Korea about the size of his "nuclear button"... "Will someone from his depleted and food starved regime please inform him that I too have a Nuclear Button, but it is a much better & more powerful one than his, and my Button works!"

Many Americans became very alarmed by these early morning outbursts and the Trump's sanity. Senator Graham said, "I feel an obligation to help him where I can. I've enjoyed working with him. I don't think he's crazy. I think he's had a very successful 2017. And I want to help him where I can. And we should all want him to be successful. He's got a lot on his plate."

.

Trump has had horrible dietary habits: 1) He loves Filet-o-Fish, Big Mac, and Quarter Pounder; 2) he washes his fast-food down with diet coke; 3) KFC fried chicken is also on his list of favorites; 4) pizza is another treat, but not the crust; 5) he usually skips breakfast or has eggs, bacon/sausage, hashbrowns and biscuits; 6) he enjoys his steak, but well done; 7) he does not drink beer, nor any alcohol; 8) he is very picky about his French fries; and 9) cheese is another favorite. However, he always found time for his golf game. Although he blamed Obama for taking a lot of time off, no President has beat his days on the green. The good news was that Trump was golfing when the Hawaii scare occurred with a false alarm on a nuclear attack.

Days at Golf Course During First 81 Days

Trump	17	███████████████
Obama	0	
Bush	0	
Clinton	3	███

CHAPTER ELEVEN: COLLUSION OR NO COLLUSION?

Until Special Prosecutor Robert Mueller makes a decision about who, if anyone, was involved with Russia's interference into the election, it is quite interesting and informative to follow the events that occurred during 2016 and 2017. Thanks to Bill Moyers and Moyers & Company for the thorough timeline of U.S. and Russia interaction and all the many, many people involved. Moyers & Company is a weekly series of interviews and ideas aimed at helping viewers make sense of the present tumultuous times through the insight of America' most astute thinkers

It's up to the readers on this book to read all that has taken place and determine their own conclusions about collusion.

2016 to 2017

Michael Flynn applied for a five-year renewal of his security clearance. When asked about his Moscow appearance, Flynn reportedly said, "I didn't take any money from Russia, if that's what you're asking me."

American petroleum industry consultant Carter Page became an unofficial volunteer to the Trump campaign as part of an informal foreign policy committee. The campaign had asked Iowa Tea Party activist Sam Clovis to line up some foreign policy advisers, and Page was on the list. Shortly after the public announcement of his affiliation with the Trump campaign, Page received an invitation to give a speech at the New Economic School in Moscow.

Flynn denied taking money from Russia.

When questions arose about Trump's relation with Russia, he changed his story: "I have no relationship with [Vladimir Putin], other than he called me a genius."

Sessions formally endorsed Trump for U.S. President. Three days later, Trump named Sessions chair of the campaign's National Security Advisory Committee.

Lobbyist Paul Manafort submitted a proposal to Trump, which contained information on how he could help him secure enough convention delegates to be nominated. Manafort described how he helped wealthy and powerful business and political leaders, including oligarths and dictators in Russia and Ukraine. "I have managed presidential campaigns around the world," he explained.

Trump narrowed the field of the Presidential race, with only Marco Rubio, Ted Cruz, and John Kasich left in the running.

George Papadopoulos, a 28-year-old DePaul University graduate, is picked by Clovis as a Trump foreign policy adviser. Clovis told Papadopoulos that a principal foreign policy focus of the campaign will be improved relations with Russia. According to *The Washington Post* , when Clovis was a candidate for the U.S. Senate in 2014, he "had questioned the effectiveness of U.S. sanctions imposed after Russia's incursion into Ukraine."

According to a report summary from U.S. Representative Elijah Cummings, Flynn told investigators he was paid by "U.S. companies" when he traveled to Moscow in December 2015 and had not received any benefit from a foreign country.

When traveling to Italy, Papadopoulos met Joseph Mifsud, a middleman between him and the Russian leadership who claimed to have strong connections with Russian officials. Papadopoulos believed that these connections could increase his importance to the Trump campaign.

In discussions about Trump's foreign policy positions, Sessions said: "I think an argument can be made there is no reason for the U.S. and Russia to be at this loggerhead. Somehow, someway we ought to be able to break that logjam. Strategically it's not justified for either country."

In an interview with *The Washington Post*, Trump identified Page and Papadopoulos as two of his foreign policy advisers. He referred to Papadopoulos by name as "an energy and oil consultant, excellent guy."

In London, Mifsud introduced Papadopoulos to someone who investigators later described as a "female Russian national" (later identified by *The New York Times* as Olga Polonskaya). Mifsud said she was Putin's niece with connections to senior Russian officials. In fact, Putin has no niece, and Polonskaya was from St. Petersburg and a former manager of a wine distribution company.

Three days after Trump identified him as a member of the foreign policy team, Papadopoulos sent an email to several campaign officials with the subject line: "Meeting with Russian Leadership — Including Putin." According to *The Washington Post*, he offered to set up "a meeting between us and the Russian leadership to discuss U.S.-Russia ties under President Trump." Papadopoulos said his Russian contacts welcomed the opportunity, because he had just met with his "good friend" (Mifsud), who introduced him to "Putin's niece." Page, whose name is also on the email, later confirmed that Mifsud was named. Clovis, who responded to the email, said he would "work it through the campaign," but that no commitments should be made at this point. "Great work," he added.

Trump hired Manafort based on the recommendation of Roger Stone, an old friend and political consultant, and Manafort joined the campaign as convention manager responsible for lining up delegates. Manafort's associate Richard Gates accompanied him and became Manafort's deputy.

Trump met with his national security team in the old U.S. Post Office, Trump Hotel, in Washington and then tweeted a photo of the participants. Those pictured included Sessions, policy advisor J.D. Gordon and Papadopoulos. Gordon later told CNN's Jim Acosta that Trump said at the meeting, "I do not want to go to World War III over Ukraine."

When Papadopoulos introduced himself, he stated he had connections to help arrange a meeting between Trump and Putin. According to Gordon, Trump "heard him out" and was intrigued by the idea. According to another attendee, Trump listened with interest and asked questions of Papadopoulos; Trump "didn't say yes, and he didn't say no."

(In a later interview, Gordon said the proposal was "ultimately shut down within a few minutes by Senator Sessions, in no uncertain terms." Asked whether Trump "shut it down," Gordon responded, "Mr. Trump's comments are something that are privileged and confidential because of the non-disclosure agreement that we all signed as part of the campaign, so I'm not going to get into his reaction. But, I will tell you he didn't say yes, that's for sure. He didn't agree with it. He didn't say yes." Gordon also said that during the campaign, "There actually were a lot of contacts with Russians," but nothing illegal. He described Papadopoulos' contacts as "maybe a bit shady, but they weren't illegal.")

(When asked at a later date about this meeting, Trump said "I don't remember much. It was a very unimportant meeting, took place a long time ago."

Despite some Trump advisers' concerns about the legality and political repercussions of a meeting between Trump and Putin (and their associates), for the next several months Papadopoulos (who reportedly told campaign officials that he was acting as an intermediary for the Russian government) sent additional emails to Trump's top campaign advisers about Russia's desire for this meeting

(During Sessions' Senate confirmations as Attorney General, he said he was "not aware" that anyone affiliated with the Trump campaign communicated with the Russian government. However, two months later, *The Washington Post* reported that Sessions spoke with the U.S. Russian Ambassador Sergey Kislyak at least twice in 2016. When questioned again, Sessions said he met with the ambassador after the Republican National Convention and then on two other occasions, but that those meetings were not relevant to the questions asked at the confirmation. Sessions then recused himself from the Russia investigation into Russian election meddling. Since he was involved in the campaign, he did not believe he should participate in this investigation. In October,

Papadopoulos pled guilty of making false statements to the FBI. The charging documents explained that Papadopoulos attended the meeting at the Trump Hotel and told Sessions "that he had connections that could help arrange a meeting between then-candidate Trump" and Putin. When asked about this, Sessions said, "I do now recall the March 31, 2016 meeting at Trump Hotel that Mr. Papadopoulos attended, but I have no clear recollection of the details of what he said during that meeting." In Washington, the Trump Campaign Foreign Policy Team members met for dinner. Papadopoulos sat next to Sessions with a group including Page, who told Sessions he was traveling to Moscow to give a speech. Other attendees may have included retired Lt. Gen. Keith Kellogg.)

Papadopoulos traveled to Greece. According to Greek officials, he was "presenting himself to officials including the Greek president and foreign minister as a senior campaign official."

Flynn and other Trump campaign advisors made at least 18 calls and emails with Russian officials. These included six contacts with Kislyak. Reuter News later reported Kushner also made at least two calls to Kislyak.

Russia extended the Trump business trademarks, which were soon to expire. Trump had originally asked for trademarks for hotel and branding ideas that were dropped.

U.S. Representative Dana Rohrabacher met with Russian legislators. According to the Russian state-sponsored propaganda network, RT, Rohrabacher expressed "his gratitude for Russia's positive role in world affairs" and blamed the deterioration of U.S.-Russian relations on the "ignorance" and "stupidity" of American politicians. "They do not give you credit for the good things you are doing."

While in Moscow, Rohrabacher met with Russian lawyer Natalia Veselnitskaya to discuss the Magnitsky Act. Veselnitskaya was one of the principal players in Russia's efforts to eliminate U.S. sanctions under the act. In a later interview, Veselnitskaya said she provided Rohrabacher with a copy of a propaganda documentary that questioned the credibility of Magnitsky Act and founder Browder. *The Daily Beast* the *Financial Times* and *The Atlantic* later added that while he was in Moscow, the Russian prosecutor general's office gave Rohrabacher a "confidential" document challenging the Western narrative leading to the Magnitsky Act. Reportedly, the document raised the prospect that repealing the law could lead to improved relations between America and Russia. Rohrabacher's itinerary did not list the meeting with Russian prosecutors. **(Rohrabacher was later interviewed by the House and Senate Intelligence Committees, and it is said that Mueller's team has wanted to do the same. Whether or not this has taken place is unknown.)**

Papadopoulos traveled to Israel to discuss Trump's Russia Policy with research associates of the Begin-Sadat Center for Strategic Studies.

Trump, said Papadopoulos, saw Putin as a responsible actor and potential partner. After all, Russia had good trade relations with European countries and even with Turkey before recent "incidents" (the Russian invasion of Crimea; the Turkish shooting down of a Russian military jet). Russia has been careful not to cross NATO lines and has been respectful of Israeli concerns in Syria and elsewhere, too.

China, added Papadopoulos, has been the emerging superpower threat. The U.S. and Russia must work to counter Chinese expansionism in Asia and the Middle East. The U.S. did not want Russia selling advanced weapon systems to China. Therefore, a policy of isolating Russia was "not sustainable. In particular, the U.S. and Russia have shared a strong interest in combating the export of radical and violent Islam from the Middle East and to stop its spread into the Muslim republics on the borders of Russia, into Europe, and into the Baltics. Papadopoulos believed that Trump could ally with Putin in this regard.

Papadopoulos continued to work with Mifsud and Polonskaya to arrange a meeting between the Trump campaign and the Russian government. He advised the campaign of his efforts, sending multiple emails to colleagues on the foreign policy team regarding his "outreach to Russia."

Papadopoulos also sent an email to Polonskaya, who responded the next day that she "would be very pleased to support" his "initiatives between our two countries."

Papadopoulos emailed back, cc'ing Mifsud about arranging "a potential foreign policy trip to Russia."

Mifsud replied, "This is already been agreed. I am flying to Moscow on the 18th for a Valdai meeting, plus other meetings at the Duma"(a legislative body in Moscow)."

Polonskaya responded, "I have already alerted my personal links to our conversation and your request… As mentioned we are all very excited by the possibility of a good relationship with Mr. Trump. The Russian Federation would love to welcome him once his candidature would be officially announced."

According to later reporting from *The Atlantic*, Manafort sent an email to Konstantin Kilimnik, a Soviet army veteran. For a decade, Kilimnik also had worked for Manafort in the Ukrainian capital. "I assume you have shown our friends my media coverage, right?"

Manafort wrote. "Absolutely," Kilimnik responded a few hours later from Kiev. "Every article."

"How do we use to get whole," Manafort asked. "Has OVD operation seen?" Apparently, the initials "OVD" referred to Oleg Deripaska, a Russian oligarch and one of Russia's richest men. A subsequent report in *The Atlantic* noted, "the source also confirmed that one of the individuals repeatedly mentioned in the email exchange as an intermediary to Deripaska is an aide to the oligarch." The emails did not specify how Manafort hoped "to get whole." (Oleg Deripaska is a Russian oligarth and philanthropist.)

Via email, Mifsud introduced Papadopoulos to Ivan Timofeev, the Moscow-based program director at a Russian government-funded think tank, the Russian International Affairs Council. (Timofeev is later described by investigators as the "Russian MFA connection.") Timofeev told Papadopoulos that he had connections with the Russian Ministry of Foreign Affairs, a Russian government entity handling foreign policy like the U.S. State Department. Papadopoulos and Timofeev then had multiple conversations over Skype and email about setting "the groundwork" for a "potential" meeting between the Trump campaign and Russian government officials.

When Trump won the New York primary and appeared to be the front-runner for the Republican nomination, Manafort assumed greater control over the Trump campaign.

The Democratic National Committee's IT department noticed suspicious computer activity, contacted the FBI and hired a private security firm, CrowdStrike, to investigate.

Timofeev sent Papadopoulos an email thanking him "for an extensive talk" and proposing "to meet in London or Moscow." Papadopoulos replied with the suggestion that "we set one up here in London with the ambassador as well as to discuss a process moving forward."

Papadopoulos emailed a person later described by investigators as a Trump campaign "senior policy adviser" — reported by *The New York Times* to be Stephen Miller: "The Russian government has an open invitation by Putin for Mr. Trump to meet when he is ready." He also wrote, "The advantage of being in London is that these   governments tend to speak a bit more openly in 'neutral' cities."

During breakfast at a London hotel, Mifsud told Papadopoulos that he had just returned from Moscow, where he met with high-level Russian government officials. Mifsud said he learned that the Russians had obtained "dirt" on Hillary Clinton. Papadopoulos later told the FBI that "the Russians had emails on Clinton"; "they have thousands of emails."

After winning Republican primaries in several states, Trump said at a victory speech, "We're going to have a great relationship with Putin and Russia."

Papadopoulos emailed a Trump senior policy adviser — **later reported by *The New York Times* to be Stephen Miller--**"Have some interesting messages coming in from Moscow about a trip when the time is right."

Trump gave his first foreign policy speech in April at the Mayflower Hotel. Before the meeting, Sessions and Russian Ambassador Kislyak attended a small VIP reception. According to report in *The Washington Post*, Kislyak told his superiors in Moscow that he and Sessions discussed campaign-related matters, including policy issues important to Moscow.

Although Kushner also met with Kislyak, he did not disclose the meeting in testimony before the Senate Intelligence Committee until a year later. He said, "We shook hands, exchanged brief pleasantries and I thanked them for attending the event and said I hoped they would like candidate Trump's speech and his ideas for a fresh approach to America's foreign policy."

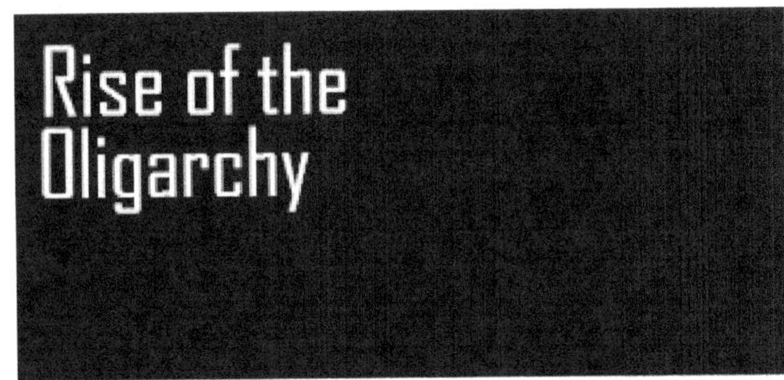

Papadopoulos sent an email to Campaign Manager Corey Lewandowski, about arranging a meeting between Trump representatives and Russian officials. "Putin wants to host the Trump team when the time is right." He also sent an email to Mifsud to thank him for his "critical help" in arranging a meeting between the Trump campaign and the Russian government. "It's history-making if it happens."

CrowdStrike determined that highly sophisticated Russian intelligence–affiliated adversaries, called Cozy Bear and Fancy Bear--were responsible for the DNC hack. Fancy Bear, in particular, had indicators of affiliation with Russia's Main Intelligence Directorate (also known as the GRU).

Timofeev sent an email to Papadopoulos and Mifsud, stating, "I have just talked to my colleagues from the MFA" (Russian Ministry of Foreign Affairs). "The[y] are open for cooperation. One of the options is to make a meeting for you and the North America desk, if you are in Moscow."

Papadopoulos responded that he was "[g]lad the MFA is interested" and forwarded the email to Lewandowski and added, "What do you think? Is this something we want to move forward with?" The next day, Papadopoulos had a phone call with Clovis and then forwarded the email from Timofeev to Clovis, adding to the top of the email: "Russia updates."

Clovis responded, "There are legal issues we need to mitigate, meeting with foreign officials as a private citizen."

Mifsud emailed Papadopoulos an "update" of their "recent discussions." Included was: "We will continue to liaise through you with the Russian counterparts in terms of what is needed for a high-level meeting of Mr. Trump with the Russian Federation."

Papadopoulos emailed Lewandowski, saying that the Russian government has "relayed to me that they are interested in hosting Mr. Trump."

\-------------------------------------

Steve Bannon, then head of Breitbart News, introduced the Trump campaign to Cambridge Analytica, a data-mining firm where he was a vice president prior to joining the campaign. The firm was backed by hedge-fund tycoon and GOP donor Robert Mercer and his daughter Rebekah. Mercer also has a multimillion-dollar investment in Breitbart. According to the firm's CEO, Andrew Nix, Cambridge Analytica had created "profiles" consisting of several thousand data points for 220 million Americans. The company specialized in "psychographic " profiling, which creates profiles of voters. **(The Trump campaign later made payments to Cambridge Analytica for "data management services.")**

\-------------------------------------

According to Federal Election Commission filings, the Ted Cruz for President Campaign had paid Cambridge Analytica over $5 million from 2015 to 2016. After Cruz withdrew from the race, the Mercers moved their support to Trump.

\-------------------------------------

The New York Times reported that Papadopoulos went drinking in London with Alexander Downer, Australia's top diplomat in Britain, and told him that the Russians have "dirt" on Hillary Clinton. Confirming the story, the *Sydney (AU) Morning Herald* reported that in July 2016, the Australian ambassador to the U.S. personally directed Papadopoulos' revelation to the FBI.

\-------------------------------------

In an email to Trump advisers Walid Phares and Gordon, Page wrote, "As discussed, my strategy in order to keep in sync with the media relations guidelines of the campaign has been to make my key messages as low-key and apolitical as possible. But after seeing the principal's tweet [presumably meaning Donald Trump's] a few hours ago in response to the cocky 'in politics and in life, ignorance is not a virtue' quote by the same speaker at Rutgers yesterday, I got another idea. If he'd like to take my place [going to Russia] and raise the temperature a little bit, of course I'd be more than happy to yield this honor to him." Page was referring to Obama's commencement speech the previous day at Rutgers University.

\-------------------------------------

After Manafort became Trump's Campaign Chairman, Papadopoulos emailed him about the Russian International Affairs Counsel's invitation that he had sent previously to Lewandowski. Along with that message with the subject line "Request from Russia to meet Mr. Trump," Papadopoulos wrote, "Russia has been eager to meet with Mr. Trump for quite some time and have been reaching out to me to discuss." **(Later, following Papadopoulos' guilty plea to the FBI, he explained that Manafort forwarded his email to Gates with the note, "Let['s] discuss. We need someone to communicate that DT is not doing these trips. It should be someone low level in the campaign so as not to send any signal.")**

\-------------------------------------

Page sent an email to Gordon and foreign policy advisor Bernadette Kilroy and said, "I'm planning to speak alongside the chairman and CEO of Sberbank as we'll both be giving commencement addresses at Moscow's New Economic School on July 8." Sberbank's CEO did not show up for the address.

\-------------------------------------

When Putin visited Greece for the first time in 2016, he was greeted by Panos Kammenos, Greece's pro-Putin defense minister who had pushed to end Russian sanctions. Meanwhile, Papadopoulos was already in Athens and, according to later reporting by *The Washington Post,* "quietly holding meetings across town and confiding in hushed tones that he was there on a sensitive mission on behalf of his boss, Donald Trump." While in Athens, Papadopoulos also met with Kammenos.

Kushner took lead of the data-driven Trump campaign efforts. "We found that Facebook and digital targeting were the most effective ways to reach the audiences," Kushner noted. "We brought in Cambridge Analytica."

In a later interview, Kushner said, "I called some of my friends from Silicon Valley who were some of the best digital marketers in the world. And I asked them how to scale this stuff. Doing it state-by-state is not that hard. But scaling is a very, very hard thing. They gave me a lot of their subcontractors, and I built in Austin a data hub that would complement the RNC's data hub. We had about 100 people in that office, which nobody knew about until toward the end. We used that as the nerve center that drove a lot of the deployment of our ground-game resources... We played *Moneyball,* where we were asking, 'Which states will be the most cost-effective — ROI per electoral vote?' We used a lot of things to get much more bang for the buck..."

Kushner added, "Take a market like Florida; we analyzed the different aspects of the state. We did our TV buying, our digital buying, our walking, our phones, all based on geography."

(According to later reporting from the publishing firm McClatchy Company, by July 2017, "Congressional and Justice Department investigators are focusing on whether Trump's campaign pointed Russian cyber operatives to certain voting jurisdictions in key states — areas where Trump's digital team and Republican operatives were spotting unexpected weakness in voter support for Hillary Clinton, according to several people familiar with the parallel inquiries.")

After winning the New Jersey primary on June 7, Trump said, "I am going to give a major speech on probably Monday of next week [June 13] and we're going to be discussing all of the things that have taken place with the Clintons. I think you're going to find it very informative and very, very interesting... Hillary Clinton turned the State Department into her private hedge fund — the Russians, the Saudis, the Chinese — all gave money to Bill and Hillary and got favorable treatment in return. It's a sad day in America when foreign governments with deep pockets have more influence in our own country than our great citizens."

June 9, 2016 meeting at Trump Tower

Rob Goldstone, a music publicist, sent Donald, Jr. an email stating that one of his clients, Russian popstar Emin Agalarov, son of Russian real estate developer Aras Agalarov, had "something very interesting" he wanted to pass along. The message said, "The Crown prosecutor of Russia met with his father Aras this morning and in their meeting offered to provide the Trump campaign with some official documents and information that would

incriminate Hillary and her dealings with Russia and would be very useful to your father. This is obviously very high level and sensitive information but is part of Russia and its government's support for Mr. Trump — helped along by Aras and Emin."

Responding to Goldstone's email, Donald, Jr. said, "If it's what you say, I love it, especially later in the summer." Four days later, Goldstone emailed Donald, Jr. again to "schedule a meeting with you and The Russian government attorney who is flying over from Moscow."

(Donald, Jr.'s explanation about this meeting was to change and change again. He first said that the meeting between himself and a Russian lawyer was primarily about "adoptions." This admission was a response to a *New York Times* piece detailing the meeting between Trump, Manafort, Kushner and Russian lawyer Veselnitskaya.

When the *Times* printed a second article about Donald, Jr.'s meeting with Veselnitskaya, who promised that she had "damaging information" about Hillary Clinton, he altered his story. "After pleasantries were exchanged, the woman stated that she had information that individuals connected to Russia were funding the Democratic National Committee and supporting Ms. Clinton," Donald, Jr. said. "Her statements were vague, ambiguous and made no sense. No details or supporting information was provided or even offered. It quickly became clear that she had no meaningful information.")

On the same day as the Trump Tower meeting, Trump tweeted about Clinton: "How long did it take your staff of 823 people to think that up--and where are your 33,000 emails that you deleted?"

According to CNN, Goldstein sent an email to Agalarov and Kaveladze, who attended the Trump Tower meeting. The email forwarded a CNN story on Russia's hacking of DNC emails. Later, in another email to senior Trump aide Dan Scavino (who became President Trump's Social Media Director) Goldstein encouraged Scavino to get Trump to create a page on the Russian social networking site Vkontakte, saying "Don and Paul" were on board with the idea.

CNN also reported, "One source says Goldstone pitched the idea to Scavino as a way to connect with the many Russian Americans who use the site. Another source said Goldstone presented it as a 'cute marketing idea,' and was passing it along for an acquaintance at the Russian social media site. That source also said Goldstone mentioned the idea after the Trump Tower meeting as everyone was leaving, though Goldstone continued to push this proposal in emails in the weeks following."

Trump's Attorney Michael Cohen received an email from Felix Sater, Russian- born American real estate developer. According to a *Washington Post* reporter, "Sater encouraged Cohen to attend the St. Petersburg International Economic Forum, with Sater telling Cohen that he could be introduced to Russian Prime Minister Dmitry Medvedev, top financial leaders and perhaps Putin, according to people familiar with the correspondence."

After Ukraine's prime minister visited Washington, House Speaker Ryan, House Majority Leader Kevin McCarthy and other Republican leaders met privately. During this session, McCarthy said, "I'll guarantee you that's what it is... The Russians hacked the DNC and got the opp [opposition] research they had on Trump." Moments later he joked, "There's two people I think Putin pays: Rohrabacher and Trump."

On June 12, during an interview on British television, WikiLeaks founder Julian Assange said that the website had obtained and would publish a batch of Clinton emails.

American spies were intercepting conversations about senior Russian intelligence and political officials. Russians discussed using Manafort and Flynn — both who had previous

Russian contacts — to shape Trump's Russian opinions. Then CIA Director Brennan noticed guarded contacts between Russian officials and Trump campaign associates. Brennan believed the American election was under attack and worried that Trump's campaign may have been supporting the effort. Brennan referred his concerns to the FBI.

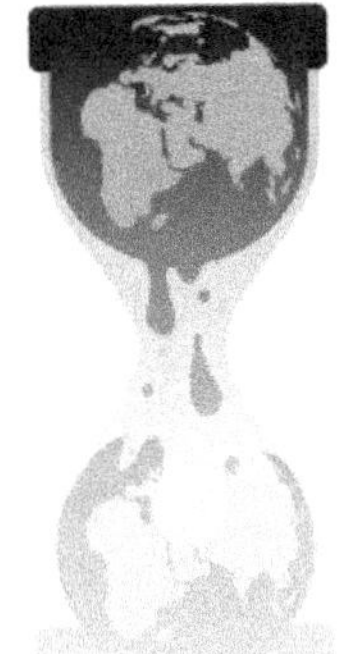

According to *Politico*, Sater visited Trump Tower on "confidential" business in July. Sater declined to answer whether he had recent contact with the Trump Organization or children. "I don't see the relevance of that," he said. When *Politico* asked the Trump campaign about Sater, the Trump spokesperson said, "We are not aware of a contribution or visit to Trump Tower."

Pence, who was in a critical re-election race for the Indiana gubernatorial election, played golf with Trump. Manafort urged Trump to choose Pence for Vice President. He was soon chosen.

FBI Director James Comey announced the bureau closed its yearlong investigation into Clinton's use of a private email server while Secretary of State. Comey said Clinton was "extremely careless" in handling "very sensitive, highly classified information" but did not recommend prosecution. Usually, when the FBI has recommended closing a case, the Justice Department has agreed, and no public statement follows. It may be that the Russians hacking of the DNC played a part in this decision.

Apparently referring to himself in third person, Page emailed Trump campaign members, "Campaign Adviser Carter Page presented before gatherings at the New Economic School, NES, in Moscow, including their 2006 commencement ceremony. Russian Deputy Prime Minister and NES Board Member Arkady Dvorkovich also spoke before the event. In a private conversation, Dvorkovich expressed strong support for Mr. Trump and a desire to work together toward devising better solutions in response to the vast range of current international problems."

Page then wrote to Trump advisors Tera Dahl and Gordon, "On a related front, I'll send you guys a readout soon regarding some incredible insights and outreach I've received from a few Russian legislators and senior members of the Presidential administration here." At the Republican National Convention the following week, Page also mentioned the trip to see Clovis.

According to *Bloomberg News*, Papadopoulos sent an email to a Kremlin-linked official stating that the Trump campaign had okayed a meeting between top members of the Trump campaign and Putin representatives. Reportedly, Papadopoulos suggested a meeting for August or September in the U.K. to include "my national chairman (person unknown) and maybe one other foreign policy adviser" and members of Putin's office and Russia's Ministry of Foreign Affairs. "It has been approved by our side," Papadopoulos wrote.

At this time, the Trump campaign was trying not to include a plank in the party platform that stipulated arming the Ukrainian popular resistance with weapons to combat Russia's 2014 intervention. Page emailed campaign foreign advisors saying, "As for the Ukraine amendment, excellent work." Almost a year later, Trump adviser Gordon told CNN he pushed for this platform change. According to CNN, "Gordon says he was simply advocating what Trump himself had expressed — that he did not wish to see major war break out over the situation in Ukraine."

According to NPR, "Diana Denman, a Republican delegate who supported arming U.S. allies in Ukraine, has told people that Trump aide J.D. Gordon said at the Republican Convention in 2016 that Trump directed him to support weakening that position in the official platform." Gordon denied the claim. (**Denman wanted to call for the U.S. to provide lethal defensive weapons to the Ukraine, which had been fighting a Russian-backed separatist insurrection. She did not see that any problems would arise with this wording, Apparently, members of Trump's campaign looked at her approach and asked that it be set aside to get it cleared; the language seemed too strong. As a result, the platform wording was changed with "softened" language--America would provide "appropriate assistance" to Ukraine and "greater coordination with NATO defense planning." It is unknown whether these changes were or were not for the benefit of Russia.)**

At a Heritage Foundation event during the Republican Convention, Sessions spoke individually with Kislyak. The two men had "substantive" discussions on matters including Trump's positions on Russia-related issues and prospects for U.S.-Russia relations in a Trump Administration.

Page and Gordon met with Kislyak. They stressed that Trump would like to improve relations with Russia. Page later testified that sanctions may have come up "in passing."

When George Stephanopoulos of NBC News asked Manafort whether any connections existed between the Trump campaign and Putin's regime, Manafort answered, "No, there are not. And, you know, there's no basis to it."

Trump tweeted: "The new joke in town is that Russia leaked the disastrous DNC emails, which should never have been written (stupid), because Putin likes me."

At a press conference, Trump said, "Russia, if you're listening, I hope you're able to find the 30,000 emails that are missing. I think you will probably be rewarded mightily by our press." He also insisted, "I never met Putin. I've never spoken to him." In a CBS News interview, he reiterated: "But I have nothing to do with Russia, nothing to do, I never met Putin, I have nothing to do with Russia whatsoever." **(Prior to the election, Trump had noted several times that he knew Putin. In 2013, for example, he said, "I do have a relationship, and I can tell you that he's very interested in what we're doing here today. He's probably very interested in what you and I are saying today, and I'm sure he's going to be seeing it in some form. But I do have a relationship with him.")**

The FBI opened an investigation into possible collusion between members of the Trump campaign and Russian operatives.

Manafort denied knowing anything about the Republican platform change. Boris Epshteyn, Trump's Russian-born adviser, spouted the Kremlin's party line by telling CNN: "Russia did not seize Crimea. We can talk about the conflict that happened between Ukraine and the Crimea... But there was no seizure by Russia. That's an incorrect statement, characterization, of what happened."

On CNN, Sessions defended Trump's approach to Russia: "This whole problem with Russia is really disastrous for America, for Russia and for the world," he said.

Trump told ABC News he was not involved in the Republican Party platform change about Russia's annexation of Crimea.

According to NBC News, high-level counterintelligence officials warned Trump and Clinton that foreign adversaries, including Russia, would likely try to spy on and infiltrate their campaigns. The officials told the candidates to alert the FBI about any suspicious foreign overtures to their campaigns.

British MI6 intelligence officer Christopher Steele formerly located in Moscow during the 1990s and director of a private intelligence-gathering firm in London, provided the Roman FBI office with memos of his research into Trump and Russia connections. Steele started researching Trump's Russian connections in June 2016 when the investigation Fusion GPS hired him.

Brennan warned the director of Russia's Federal Security Service not to meddle in the election.

Page's ongoing public criticism of U.S. sanctions against Russia over its actions in Ukraine and his praise for Putin generated increasing concern. A Trump campaign spokesperson described Page as an "informal policy adviser" who "does not speak for Mr. Trump or the campaign." Later, the FBI believed Page was no longer part of the Trump campaign and obtained a Federal Intelligence Surveillance Act (FISA) warrant to monitor his communications. **(In 2017, the Republicans began to make this FISA warrant into a major issue, saying that another investigation should be started. They did not believe that Page should have been monitored; the FBI was asserting too much power.)**

Stone told a conference of Florida Republicans, "I actually have communicated with Assange, of WikiLeaks."

. ------------------------------------

According to *The Washington Post*, the CIA informed Obama that based on Russian intelligence sources, Putin had given Russian officials specific objectives for the ongoing cyberattack on the U.S. election: defeat or at least to damage Clinton and help elect Trump.

Florida GOP consultant Aaron Nevins contacted hacker Guccifer 2.0, who had invited journalists to send questions via Twitter relating to information about hacking the DNC and the DCCC. Nevins began posting links to Guccifer 2.0 and said that releasing fresher data would have more impact, and the hacker should "feel free to send any Florida-based information."

After receiving complaints about the publication of private information, Guccifer 2.0 was suspended by its hosts Twitter and WordPress, Stone then tweeted, "Now Guccifer 2.0 — why are those exposing the truth banned?"

Without explanation, Twitter reinstated the Guccifer 2.0 account. In a private message to Guccifer 2.0, Stone wrote, "Delighted you are reinstated. Fuck the State and their MSM lackeys."

After several weeks of communication from Papadopoulos to other Trump campaign officials about a potential "off-the-record" meeting with Russian officials, Clovis told Papadopoulos, "I would encourage you" and another foreign policy adviser to the campaign to "make the trip... if it is feasible."

. -------------------------------------

As reports of Manafort's financial connections to Ukraine intensified, he resigned from the Trump campaign. However, Manafort's close associate, Gates, moved to the RNC and remained in Trump's inner circle of campaign advisers.

. -------------------------------------

According to the *Wall Street Journal,* wealthy GOP operative Peter W. Smith set out to get hold of any emails that were stolen from the private email server that Clinton used as Secretary of State. He assembled a team of technology experts, lawyers and a Russian-speaking investigator in Europe to help find the emails. They identified five groups of hackers, two of which were Russian. Smith claimed to be in contact with Flynn. He shared a packet of opposition research articles listing Trump campaign officials Bannon, Conway and Clovis. Responding about his effort, a Trump campaign official said Smith did not work for the campaign; if Flynn coordinated with Smith, it was as a private individual. Bannon said he never heard of Smith. Conway said she knew Smith from Republican politics but never met with him during the campaign.

. -------------------------------------

Kislyak's asked Sessions to meet with him in his Senate office. Also attending were two of Sessions' senior defense specialists. During the conversation, Kislyak argued that Russia had done nothing wrong in Ukraine.

. -------------------------------------

Senior members of the Obama administration met with 12 key congressional leaders for help with Russian interference. The response became partisan, with Democrats wanting to alert the public about Russia's efforts and Republicans dissenting. According to *The Washington Post,* McConnell voiced skepticism about whether the underlying intelligence truly supported the White House's claims about Russian interference.

Through Twitter, WikiLeaks wrote to Donald, Jr., "A PAC-run anti-Trump site 'putintrump.org' is about to launch. The PAC is a recycled pro-Iraq war PAC. We have guessed the password. It is 'putintrump'. See 'About' for who is behind it. Any comments?"

Donald, Jr. responded, "Off the record I don't know who that is, but I'll ask around. Thanks." According to *The Atlantic,* Donald, Jr. then emailed senior campaign officials, including Bannon, Conway, Brad Parscale and Kushner, saying that WikiLeaks had made contact. Kushner forwarded the email to Hicks in White House communications.

. -------------------------------------

Because the White House was not informing the public about Russian cyberattacks on the election, Senator Dianne Feinstein and Representative Adam Schiff issued a statement about Russia directing a campaign to undermine the election.

. -------------------------------------

Yahoo News reported U.S. intelligence officials were seeking to determine whether Page opened up private communications with senior Russian officials, including talks about the possibility of lifting economic sanctions if Trump became President.

Page wrote to Comey that in 2016 he did not meet "with any sanctioned official in Russia." He also said that during August 2016 he sold "at a loss" all of his holdings in Russia's majority state-owned energy giant, Gazprom. "Although I have not been contacted by any member of your team in recent months," Page concluded, "I would eagerly await their call to discuss any final questions they might possibly have in the interest of helping them put these outrageous allegations to rest while allowing each of us to shift our attention to relevant matters."

. -------------------------------------

Comey appeared before the House Judiciary Committee and refused to answer questions about whether the FBI was investigating connections between members of the Trump campaign and Russia. "We do not confirm or deny investigations," Comey said.

. -------------------------------------

Kushner's real estate company finalized a $285 million loan with Deutsche Bank as part of a refinancing package for its property near Times Square. Kushner's company received $74 million more than it paid for the property in 2015, when it had negotiated the purchase with Lev Leviev. According to the *New York Times*, Leviev — a Uzbek-born Israeli citizen who is one of the world's wealthiest men, described Putin as a "true friend" who helped him with an influential Russian Jewish organization. At the time of the refinancing, Deutsche Bank was negotiating to settle New York State regulators' charges that it aided a possible Russian money laundering scheme.

. -------------------------------------

WikiLeaks sent a private message to Donald, Jr. through Twitter: "Hiya, it'd be great if you guys could comment on/push this story," attached a quote from Clinton about wanting to "just drone" Assange. Donald, Jr. responded, "Already did that earlier today. It's amazing what she can get away with." He then added, "What's behind this Wednesday leak I keep reading about?"

. -------------------------------------

The Obama Administration Department of Homeland Security and the Director of National Intelligence James Clapper formally announced, "The US Intelligence Community (USIC) is confident that the Russian government directed the recent compromises of emails from U.S. persons and institutions, including from U.S. political organizations... We believe, based on the scope and sensitivity of these efforts, that only Russia's senior-most officials could have authorized these activities."

. -------------------------------------

Top intelligence officials of the Obama Administration announced their belief that the Russian government was behind the hacking of the DNC. Then *The Washington Post* published the "Access Hollywood" tape in which Donald Trump bragged about physically forcing himself on women. This was followed by WikiLeaks dumping myriad emails from the Clinton campaign, which had been hacked from Podesta's account.. The timing of these events have been considered essential to this investigation.

. -------------------------------------

At a campaign rally in Pennsylvania, Trump said, "I love WikiLeaks." Between October 10 and November 8, he mentioned WikiLeaks over 130 times.

. -------------------------------------

Fox & Friends anchor Steve Doocy told Pence, "Some have suggested on the left — all this bad stuff about Hillary, nothing bad about Trump, that your campaign is in cahoots with WikiLeaks." Pence answered, "Nothing could be further from the truth."

. -------------------------------------

During the third Presidential debate, Trump dismissed the U.S. intelligence findings: "[Clinton] has no idea whether it is Russia, China or anybody else... Our country has no idea." And he added: "I don't know Putin. I have no idea... I never met Putin. This is not my best friend."

. ------------------------------------

WikiLeaks' Twitter account sent Donald, Trump Jr. another private message: "Hey Don. We have an unusual idea. Leak us one or more of your father's tax returns." Reported by *The Atlantic*, "WikiLeaks then laid out three reasons why this would benefit both the Trumps and WikiLeaks. One, *The New York Times* had already published a fragment of Trump's tax returns on October 1; two, the rest could come out any time 'through the most biased source, such as *The New York Times* or MSNBC.

"It is the third reason, though, " WikiLeaks wrote, "that 'is the real kicker.' If we publish them it will dramatically improve the perception of our impartiality. That means that the vast amount of stuff that we are publishing on Clinton will have much higher impact, because it won't be perceived as coming from a 'pro-Trump' 'pro-Russia' source." An email address and link were provided where the Trump campaign could send the tax returns, and added, "The same for any other negative stuff (documents, recordings) that you think has a decent chance of coming out. Let us put it out.'"

. ------------------------------------

According to reports by MSNBC's Rachel Maddow, the $100 million plane belonging to the Russian oligarch Rybolovlev, who had bought a Florida residence from Trump for $95 million in 2008, was in Las Vegas on the same day Trump was holding a rally there. He was also in North Carolina during a Trump rally.

. ------------------------------------

Asked about news reports that the FBI was investigating connections between the Trump campaign and Russia, former campaign manager Manafort said, "None of it is true... There's no investigation going on by the FBI that I'm aware of."

. ------------------------------------

Mother Jones reporter David Corn published an article discussing some of the claims in what was called the "Steele dossier." His principal, an anonymous source for the piece, turned out to be Christopher Steele.

. ------------------------------------

In a letter to Congress leaders, Comey confirmed that the FBI had completed its review of the additional Clinton staffer Huma Mahmood Abedin emails and was still not going to prosecute Clinton for her use of a private email server.

Participating in a panel discussion at the Federation of Hellenic Societies of Greater New York on what Trump as President would mean for Greece and Cyprus, Papadopoulos stated, in Greek, "Mr. Trump and our team thought that it is very important for me to come here and talk to the Federation."

. ------------------------------------

Trump and Pence were elected.

. ------------------------------------

Putin announced Trump's election victory, and Russia's Parliament erupted in applause.

. ------------------------------------

According to *The New York Times*, Sergei Millian, a Belarusan-American businessman and onetime Russian government translator, proposed to Papadopoulos that they form an energy-related business to be financed by Russian billionaires "who are not under sanctions" and would "open all doors for us" at "any level all the way to the top." Millian stated that one billionaire wanted to explore the idea of opening a Trump-branded hotel in Moscow: "I know the President will distance himself from business, but his children might be interested." At the end of the year, Millian and Papadopoulos exchanged New Year's greetings.

. -------------------------------------

In an op-ed in *The Hill*, Flynn called Fethullah Gülen, a Muslim cleric who Turkey's President Erdoğan had accused of planning a failed coup attempt, "a shady Islamic mullah residing in Pennsylvania whom former President Clinton once called his 'friend' in a well circulated video. Gülen portrays himself as a moderate, but he is in fact a radical Islamist. He has publicly boasted about his 'soldiers' waiting for his orders to do whatever he directs them to do. If he were in reality a moderate, he would not be in exile, nor would he excite the animus of Recep Tayyip Erdoğan and his government."

Flynn continued, "Gülen's vast global network has all the right markings to fit the description of a dangerous sleeper terror network. From Turkey's point of view, Washington is harboring Turkey's Osama bin Laden."

Russia's Deputy Foreign Minister Ryabkov stated that during the campaign, the Kremlin had continued communications with Trump's "immediate entourage." Trump spokesperson Hicks denied the claim, saying that the campaign had "no contact with Russian officials" before the election.

. -----------------------------------

During their first meeting after the election, Obama warned Trump against appointing Flynn to a top national security post. In 2014, Obama had removed Flynn as the head of the Defense Intelligence Agency.

. -----------------------------------

Rykov published the first of two Facebook posts claiming he had colluded with the Trump campaign and Cambridge Analytica to swing the election in Trump's favor.

. -----------------------------------

Congressman Cummings, ranking member of the House Committee on Oversight and Government Reform, sent the Trump Transition Team Chair Pence a letter that expressed concern about Flynn's conflicts of interest. Specifically, Cummings worried about Flynn's work for an entity affiliated with Turkey and a paid trip to Moscow in December 2015 when he was "highly critical of the United States."

. -----------------------------------

Flynn was named National Security Advisor. McFarland was named senior member of his Presidential transition team and deputy national security adviser under Flynn.

. -----------------------------------

In a meeting with senior Trump transition national security team members, Flynn revealed he had scheduled a conversation with Kislyak. Marshall Billingslea, a member of the team who had been a senior Pentagon official for President George W. Bush, warned Flynn that any such communication carried risks because U.S. intelligence agencies were almost certainly monitoring Kislyak's conversations. After the meeting, Billingslea asked national security officials in the Obama White House for a copy of the classified CIA profile of Kislyak.

. -----------------------------------

Kislyak visited Trump Tower to meet with Kushner and Flynn. According to *The Washington Post*, Kislyak reported to his Russian superiors that Kushner made a surprising suggestion: Use Russia's diplomatic facilities in the U.S. for a secret and secure communications channel between Trump and the Kremlin prior to the inauguration. According to *The Post*, Kushner wanted to use the Russian embassy so that American officials could not monitor the discussions.

. -------------------------------------

Steele sent his research findings about the Trump-Russia connections to Senator John McCain, who personally delivered a copy to Comey. McCain confirmed he had done so.

. -------------------------------------

In response to a *Washington Post* report on how the CIA had concluded that Russia intervened in the election to help Trump win, Trump said, "These are the same people that said Saddam Hussein had weapons of mass destruction. The election ended a long time ago in one of the biggest Electoral College victories in history. It's now time to move on and 'Make America Great Again."

. -------------------------------------

Trump praised Rex Tillerson, chairman of ExxonMobil and recipient of Russia's "Order of Friendship" Medal from Putin in 2013, as "much more than a business executive" and a "world-class player." Trump said Tillerson "knows many of the players" and did "massive deals in Russia" for Exxon. Two days later, Trump nominated him to be Secretary of State.

. -------------------------------------

Secretary of Education Devos' brother, Erik Prince, met secretly in the Seychelles Islands with Drnitriev.

Right before his inauguration, for the first of many times, Trump called the Steele Dossier "fake news." He stated, "I think it's a disgrace that information would be let out."

2017 to 2018

Trump actually tweeted, "As Far as Hacking, I Think It Was Russia. But I think we also get hacked by other countries and other people."

. -------------------------------------

Then Press Secretary Spicer explained that Flynn's December 29 conversation with Kislyak was about "logistical information" for a meeting with Putin and Trump after the inauguration.

. -------------------------------------

Page communicated with Jones Day LLP, counsel for the Trump campaign and White House counsel, and was told he should not portray himself as a representative of the Trump campaign.

. -------------------------------------

In a CBS interview, Pence stated that Flynn's call to the Russian ambassador on the same day President Obama announced new sanctions was "strictly coincidental." He said, "They did not discuss anything having to do with the United States' decision to expel diplomats or impose censure on Russia." On Fox News, Pence denied any contact between Russia and the Trump campaign. "All the contacts by the Trump campaign and associates were with the American people."

.   ------------------------------------
        On Inauguration Day, Millian attended several VIP events for Trump supporters, including a reception for Chief of Staff Priebus.
.   ------------------------------------
        Flynn announced that Trump will "rip up" Russian sanctions. He reported that a planned nuclear power project with Russia was "good to go."
.   ------------------------------------
        Gates, Manafort's associate, helped run the inauguration celebration on the bequest of investor Thomas Barrack.
.   ------------------------------------
        The FBI was concerned that key Russians attended Trump's inauguration events. These included Natalia Veselnitskaya and Rinat Akhmetshin.
.   ------------------------------------
        Greek Defense Minister Panos Kammenos called Papadopoulos a "Trump Advisor," when they met. Two days later, Papadopoulos met with a group of Israelis leading the country's resettlement movement on the West Bank.
.   ------------------------------------
        Flynn was sworn in as National Security Advisor, which did not require Senate approval. A few days later, Spicer denied Flynn talked sanctions with Kislyak.
.   ------------------------------------
        Trump considered lifting Russian sanctions and allowing Americans to borrow from and provide financing to the Russian bank, VEB.
.   ------------------------------------
        Papadopoulos lied to the FBI during a voluntary interview about Russian interference in the election. He admitted to communications with Mifsud, but claimed these occurred before he was part of the Trump campaign team.
.   ------------------------------------
        According to Comey, Trump asked him if he would like to stay on with the FBI. Comey was confused about this comment, since Trump had earlier said he wanted Comey to remain in his present role. A number of days later, Comey told Priebus that there was a policy barring discussions between the White House and the FBI regarding ongoing investigations.
.   ------------------------------------
        Deutsche Bank, which had given the Trump organization billions of dollars of loans, agreed to pay a $425 million fine for money laundering as much as $10 billion through its Moscow, London and New York offices.
.   ------------------------------------
        Cohen, met with Sater and Andrey Artemenko, a pro-Putin lawmaker from Ukraine. Artemenko, and Sater gave Cohen a peace plan in which Russia would lease the Crimea for 50 or 100 years and, eventually, get relief from U.S. sanctions.
        Rod Rosenstein was named Justice Department Deputy Attorney General, replacing Sally Yates who was fired for not supporting Trump's travel ban. Yates had informed the White House that, based on statements by individuals such as Pence, Flynn had lied about his late-December conversations with Kislyak. Yates also told White House counsel that Flynn's lies made him vulnerable to Russian blackmail.
.   ------------------------------------
        The FBI warned Hicks about being regularly contacted through email by Russian operatives during the Presidential transition.
.   ------------------------------------

Sessions, who previously was the chair of the Trump campaign's National Security Advisory Committee, received confirmation as U.S. Attorney General.

. ------------------------------------

Flynn waivered about conversations with the Russian ambassador and sanctions. Trump told reporters he was not aware of these conversations. Flynn resigned several days later. Trump continued to call Flynn a "wonderful man," who "has been treated very, very unfairly by the media."

. ------------------------------------

At the beginning of February, as Trump was planning to go to Mar-a-Lago for the weekend, Russia oligarth Rybolovlev flew from France to Miami International airport. This was the Russian who had also previously purchased a Florida residence from Trump for $95 million in 2008. Yet, Spicer continued to deny there were any contacts between the Trump campaign and Russia.

Trump and Comey

According to Comey, on January 27 at the end of an Oval Office meeting with Pence, Sessions, Kushner and Comey, Trump asked everyone to leave except for Comey. When the two were walking out of the room, Trump said, "I want to talk about Mike Flynn" and then told Comey that Flynn did nothing wrong in speaking to the Russians; Flynn was fired because he had misled Pence. Trump then turned to the subject of leaks and the importance of keeping classified information classified and said, "I hope you can see your way clear to letting this go, to letting Flynn go. He is a good guy. I hope you can let this go." As soon as Comey left the White House, he documented the conversation.

Comey then asked Sessions to prevent any further direct communication between him and Trump. He told him about the closed meeting at the White House and said Sessions should not have been asked to leave. According to Comey, Sessions did not respond to this concern. Trump's lack of understanding about the proper way to communicate/not to communicate with the FBI continued. Priebus then asked McCabe to publicly refute a *New York Times* article about the Trump aides' Russian contacts.

Comey met privately with the Senate Intelligence Committee to discuss the Russia investigation. The committee then sent a letter to scores of agencies, organizations and individuals, as well as the White House, to preserve all communications related to the Senate's investigation on Russian interference into the 2016 election.

Without Trump's knowledge, Sessions recused himself from the Russian investigation. Public pressure was building for Sessions to step aside, because he had been a senior member of the Trump campaign. However, White House counsel, McGahn, followed the President's orders and unsuccessfully asked Sessions to remain in charge of the investigation.

Close to a month later, Trump erupted against McGahn, Bannon, Priebus, Spicer, Kushner, Ivanka Trump, and Communications Director Mike Dubke because of Sessions' recusal.

CENTRAL INTELLIGENCE AGENCY

Donald, Jr. denied involvement with any campaign-related meetings with the Russians. "Did I meet with people that were Russian? I'm sure, I'm sure I did. But none that were set up. None that I can think of at the moment. And certainly none that I was representing the campaign in any way." Sessions also denied any pre-election connections with Russians to discuss campaign issues.

Despite their earlier denials, advisors Page and Gordon admitted they met with Kislyak during the campaign.

The New York Times, and the White House confirmed, that Flynn and Kushner met with Kislyak in December 2016 to "establish a line of communication between the new administration and the Russian government."

Trump said he learned about Obama wiretapping his phones from a Fox News story. He also insisted that he had "a lot" of evidence and promised "very interesting items" will soon emerge. Comey asked the Justice Department to publicly deny false wiretapping claims. Eventually, the Intelligence Committee said these claims were false. Trump, however, would not accept these reports and continued to claim evidence would come.

WikiLeaks released myriad CIA documents about its hacking tools for smartphones, computers and Internet-connected devices. British politician Nigel Farage met with Assange at the Ecuador Embassy in London, where Assange had been seeking sanctuary since 2012. The White House made no comment about the meeting nor whether Farage was delivering a message from Trump.

Flynn disclosed the $530,000 he received between August 2016 and the Presidential election for his lobbying efforts for a Turkish company. Pence said he had no knowledge about Flynn's Turkey lobbying work.

Trump fired 46 Obama-era Justice Department U.S. attorneys including Bharara, who was surprised since Trump had recently praised him. Rosenstein and Boente remained, and still remain, the only prosecutors' left. Rosenstein became Deputy Attorney General.

These firings came a day after Fox News said Trump needed to "purge" Obama holdovers from the federal government. Commentator Sean Hannity portrayed them as "saboteurs" from the "deep state" who were leaking harmful secrets.

Trump tweeted that the House Intelligence Committee should investigate Bill and Hillary Clintons' ties to Russia.

The New York Times reported an undisclosed meeting in December 2016 between Kushner and Russian Banker Sergey Gorkov, who helped financed the construction of the President's 65-story Trump International Hotel and Tower in Toronto.

. Senator Nunes reported on an intelligence report that showed how Trump and his associates were incidentally swept up in foreign surveillance by American spy agencies. However, it was later concluded that Nunes' sources for this information was the White House. Nunes later recused himself from the Russia Investigation. However, overtime, his actions proved differently. Several months later, Nunes forced the release of a controversial and unverified memo in order to prove, he said, the case against the FBI.

Flynn offered to testify before the congressional intelligence committees in exchange of immunity. Trump sent a message to Flynn to "stay strong."

Trump and Comey Again

On May 9, Trump fired Comey, ending several months of anger and frustration. The first dismissal letter, written with political advisor Miller was opposed by White House counsel McGahn: The letter appeared too angry and meandering. It also referred to private conversations between Trump and Comey, including the time when the FBI Director told Trump he was not under investigation. Rosenstein then drafted his own letter, which Trump used as a rationale for the firing: Comey had mishandled the investigation into Hillary Clinton's private email server..That same evening, Spicer said Trump arrived at his decision after receiving a memo from Rosenstein.

In the morning, Trump tweeted that Democrats have wanted Comey fired for a while and are now faking their anger. "Comey lost the confidence of almost everyone in Washington, Republican and Democrat alike. When things calm down. they will be thanking me!" Later, when seeing former Secretary of State Henry Kissinger, Trump said he fired Comey "because he wasn't doing a good job."

Next, Deputy Press Secretary Sarah Huckabee Sanders stated that Comey committed "basic atrocities" by going around the Justice Department's chain of command and speaking out during the Clinton email investigation. She added that Trump had considered letting Comey go as early as Election Day and the FBI had lost confidence in him. Acting FBI Director McCabe, however, told members of the Senate Intelligence Committee that this was not true. Comey had "broad support" among the FBI's employees

In an interview with NBC News, Trump said he already decided to fire Comey before receiving Rosenstein's recommendation and he was thinking of "this Russia thing" when making his decision. "When I decided to do it, I said to myself, I said 'you know, this Russia thing with Trump and Russia is a made-up story. It's an excuse by the Democrats for having lost an election that they should have won.'"

Comey wrote a memo that explained how Trump asked him to end the investigation into Flynn, because he was so disgusted by the request that he wanted to document it. Comey shared the memo with senior FBI officials.

To complicate the situation more, Pence said that Comey's firing took place because Sessions and Rosenstein recommended it. Then, Sanders said Trump had been considering this firing "since the day he was elected," but Sessions and Rosenstein were "absolutely" the reason for the end result. *The Washington Post* and *New York Times* subsequently reported that Trump had been the impetus for Comey's firing, not Sessions and Rosenstein.

Rosenstein then insisted that the White House correct the false impression that he initiated the Comey firing. He could not work in an environment where facts were reported inaccurately. The White House released another timeline of Comey's firing. It said Trump was the impetus, not Rosenstein. However, it also said Trump met with Sessions and Rosenstein to discuss "reasons for removing the director."

Further, in an interview with NBC's Lester Holt, Trump said, "Regardless of any recommendations, I was going to fire Comey, knowing there was no good time to do it. And in fact, when I decided to do it, I said to myself, I said, 'You know, this Russia thing with Trump and Russia is a made up story....'" Later in the interview, Trump said that on three different occasions — once in person and twice over the phone — he had asked Comey if he (Donald Trump) was under investigation for alleged ties to Russia, and Comey told him he was not.

Worried about conflicting stories between him and Comey, Trump tweeted: "James Comey better hope there are no 'tapes' of our conversations before he leaks to the press." This tweet stirred up a hornet's nest. Spicer refused to answer questions on whether Trump was taping Oval Office conversations. This was never substantiated.

A couple of days later, Trump met with Kislyak and Foreign Minister Lavrov and told them, "I just fired the head of the FBI. He was crazy, a real nut job. I faced great pressure because of Russia. That's taken off. I am not under investigation." *The Washington Post* reported that Trump revealed highly classified information on the Islamic State to the Russian foreign minister and ambassador in this Oval Office meeting. The information had been provided to Trump through an intelligence sharing agreement, "considered so sensitive that details have been withheld from allies and tightly restricted even within the U.S. government, officials said." Putin then offered to provide the U.S. Congress with transcripts of the Oval Office conversations. National Security Advisor McMaster said this exchange of information was not of importance.

On May 17, Rosenstein named former FBI Director Robert Mueller as special counsel to oversee the FBI's investigation into Russian interference with the election. In a White House statement, Trump said, "As I have stated many times, a thorough investigation will confirm what we already know — there was no collusion between my campaign and any foreign entity. I look forward to this matter concluding quickly."

Two days later, Trump tweeted: "This is the single greatest witch hunt of a politician in American history," and "With all the illegal acts that took place in the Clinton campaign &Obama Administration, there never was a special counsel appointed!" The White House tried to undermine Mueller's excellent reputation, focusing on a rule that restricted newly hired government lawyers from investigating clients of their former employer for at least one year. Trump had already extended that to two years by Executive Order, but the Justice Department could waive the rule. Further, although Trump wanted Mueller to be fired, White House counsel McGahn threatened to resign if he did so.

The Department of Homeland Security reported that individuals connected to the Russian government tried to hack election-related computer systems in 21 U.S. states. However, the White House continued lobbying the House of Representatives to weaken the Senate bill that would limit Trump's power to curtail Russian sanctions.

Donald, Jr.'s June Meeting Again

While *The New York Times* readied its own report on Donald, Jr.'s June 2016 meeting, Donald, Jr. released more information about his own information. "It was a short introductory meeting. I asked Jared and Paul to stop by. We primarily discussed a program about the adoption of Russian children that was active and popular with American families years ago, and was since ended by the Russian government, but it was not a campaign issue at the time and there was no follow-up... I was asked to attend the meeting by an acquaintance, but was not told the name of the person I would be meeting with beforehand."

A spokesman for Trump's legal team instead added, "We have learned from both our own investigation and public reports that the participants in the meeting misrepresented who they were and who they worked for. Specifically, we have learned that the person who sought the meeting is associated with Fusion GPS, a firm which according to public reports, was retained by Democratic operatives to develop opposition research on the President and which commissioned the phony Steele dossier."

Donald, Jr. revised his story: "I was asked to have a meeting by an acquaintance I knew from the 2013 Miss Universe pageant with an individual who I was told might have information helpful to the campaign. I was not told her name prior to the meeting. I asked Jared and Paul to attend, but told them nothing of the substance. We had a meeting in June 2016.

"After pleasantries were exchanged, the woman stated that she had information that individuals connected to Russia were funding the Democratic National Committee and supporting Ms. Clinton. Her statements were vague, ambiguous and made no sense. No details or supporting information was provided or even offered. It quickly became clear that she had no meaningful information. She then changed subjects and began discussing the adoption of Russian children and mentioned the Magnitsky Act.

"It became clear to me that this was the true agenda all along and that the claims of potentially helpful information were a pretext for the meeting. I interrupted and advised her that my father was not an elected official, but rather a private citizen, and that her comments and concerns were better addressed if and when he held public office. The meeting lasted approximately 20 to 30 minutes. As it ended, my acquaintance apologized for taking up our time. That was the end of it and there was no further contact or follow-up of any kind. My father knew nothing of the meeting or these events."

Days later, WikiLeaks sent Donald, Jr. this message: "Hi Don. Sorry to hear about your problems. We have an idea that may help a little. We are VERY interested in confidentially obtaining and publishing a copy of the email(s) cited in the *NY Times* today. We think this is strongly in your interest. Why? Because otherwise your opponents (who clearly have a copy) will gradually 'milk' phrases from the email(s) with their own spin/context added according to what suits THEIR timing and THEIR strategy over days/weeks/months. Us publishing not only deprives them of this ability but is beautifully confounding." Later that day, Donald, Jr. posted the emails himself through Twitter.

The New York Times reported that Trump signed off on his son's initial and false statement about the June meeting. Trump lawyer Jay Sekulow said on an interview with ABC that the *Times* story was incorrect. "The President didn't sign off on anything. He was coming back from the G20, the statement that was released on Saturday was released by Donald Trump, Jr. and, I'm sure, in consultation with his lawyers. The President wasn't involved in that."

In addition, Trump told Reuters that he had only recently learned about the June meeting: "I didn't know until a couple of days ago when I heard about this."

Trump repeated that assertion while speaking with reporters that night. "I only heard about it two or three days ago. In fact maybe it was mentioned at some point." However, he denied that the meeting was about sharing "dirt" on Hillary Clinton. To the contrary, Yahoo News reported that Trump's legal team had known more than three weeks earlier about the meeting.

NBC News next reported, "The Russian lawyer who met with Donald Trump, Jr. and others on the Trump team after a promise of compromising material on Hillary Clinton was accompanied by a Russian-American lobbyist — a former Soviet counterintelligence officer who is suspected by some U.S. officials of having ongoing ties to Russian intelligence." The lobbyist, Rinat Akhmetshin, told the Associated Press that he attended the meeting, and the Russian lawyer Natalia Veselnitskaya presented Trump associates with details of what supposed illicit funds had been funneled to the DNC. She suggested that making the information public could help the Trump campaign. "This could be a good issue to expose how the DNC is accepting bad money." He said Veselnitskaya carried a plastic folder with documents but was not sure whether they were provided by the Russian government nor if she left the materials with a Trump associate.

Trump's lawyer Sekulow told NBC about Donald, Jr.'s description of the meeting: "I do want to be clear — that the President was not involved in the drafting of the statement and did not issue the statement. It came from Donald, Jr. So that's what I can tell you, because that's what we know. And Donald Trump Jr. has said the same thing."

The President tweeted: "Most politicians would have gone to a meeting like the one Don, jr attended in order to get info on an opponent. That's politics!" Then, Spicer reiterated the comments about the Magnitsky Act and adoption ban of Russian children. "There was nothing, as far as we know, that would lead anyone to believe that there was anything except for a discussion about adoption and the Magnitsky Act."

CNN and *The Washington Post* reported on another person who attended the June meeting: Ike Kaveladze, Aras Agalarov's associate and vice president, who focused on real estate and finance for Crocus Group.

Sometime later, Trump told *The New York Times*: "As I've said — most other people, you know, when they call up and say, 'By the way, we have information on your opponent,' I think most politicians — I was just with a lot of people, they said [inaudible], 'Who wouldn't have taken a meeting like that?"

Trump repeated he did not know about the meeting in advance: "Well, I never saw the email. I never saw the email until, you know —" When asked if he knew about the meeting at

the time, Trump says, "No, I didn't know anything about the meeting... No, nobody told me. I didn't know nothing — It's a very unimportant — sounded like a very unimportant meeting."

Trump's anger about not having enough control about the Russian investigation grew: "Sessions should have never recused himself, and if he was going to recuse himself, he should have told me before he took the job, and I would have picked somebody else," he expressed strongly.

The New York Times and *The Washington Post* reported that Trump's lawyers were investigating ways to limit or block Mueller's investigation, including possible conflicts of interest with members of Mueller's legal team and the President's power to pardon associates, family members and even himself. One of Trump's attorneys responded that these articles are "nonsense."

An interview with *The Wall Street Journal* became public about a month later where Trump is asked if Mueller's job is safe: ""We're going to see. I mean, I have no comment yet, because it's too early. But we'll see. We're going to see. Here's the good news: I was never involved with Russia. There was nobody in the campaign. I've got 200 people that will say that they've never seen anybody on the campaign... There's nobody on the campaign that saw anybody from Russia. We had nothing to do with Russia... And if Jeff Sessions didn't recuse himself, we wouldn't even be talking about this subject."

FBI agents executed a search warrant at Manafort's home under Mueller's direction.

Papadopoulos was arrested and pleaded guilty of lying to federal agents working for Mueller.

The Washington Post reported that the President dictated a misleading statement for his son to describe the meeting with the Russians in June. "The President directed that Trump Jr.'s statement to *The Times* describe that meeting as unimportant. He wanted the statement to say that the meeting had been initiated by the Russian lawyer and primarily was about her pet issue — the adoption of Russian children." Responding to the article, Trump's lawyer said, "Apart from being of no consequence, the [*Post's*] characterizations are misinformed, inaccurate and not pertinent."

Sanders said, "The statement that Don, Jr. issued is true. There's no inaccuracy in the statement. The President weighed in as any father would, based on the limited information that he had."

Trump called Senator Thom Tillis who was co-sponsoring legislation that would limit the President's ability to fire Mueller. Trump's call to McConnell ended up in a shouting match. Trump was upset about the healthcare bill, but even more so that McConnell had not protected him from the Russian investigation. Later in the month, Trump lobbied Senator Roy Blunt to "wrap up" the investigation and prodded other legislators to push Senator Richard Burr to end it. An investigation into Clinton's connection with the intelligence-gathering firm Fusion GPS was then started by the Republicans.

Manafort and Gates were indicted by the Mueller investigation. They faced 12 counts, including conspiracy to launder money, being unregistered agents of a foreign principal, and false and misleading Foreign Agents Registration Unit statements.

Flynn continued to distance himself from the White House and Trump. and then pled guilty to making false statements to the FBI about conversations with Russian Officials on sanctions and the U.N. vote to condemn Israeli settlements. Flynn also admitted to false statements in filings under the Foreign Agents Registration Act relating to his work.

Trump asked Rosenstein where the Russian investigation was headed and whether he was "on my team." Rosenstein noted, "Of course, we're all on your team, Mr. President." However, when Trump's lawyers demanded a new special counsel be hired to investigate Mueller's conflict of interest. Rosenstein supported Mueller's investigation. It was "not a witch hunt... I believe based on his reputation, his service, his patriotism and his experience with the department and with the FBI, I believe he was an ideal choice for this task."

Rumors started flying about Trump's desire to fire Rosenstein and then Mueller. Trump denied this and numerous times said, "There is no collusion." Trump continued to attack Mueller as "reckless, inappropriate" and "extremely worrying...Beyond being irresponsible, the seemingly coordinated nature of these claims should alarm us all. Particularly since, in recent days, these baseless accusations have been repeated by several members of the House of Representatives."

Senator Warner called on all Senators to "make a clear and unambiguous statement

that any attempt by this president to remove special counsel Mueller from his position, or to pardon key witnesses in any effort to shield them from accountability or shut down the investigation would be a gross abuse of power and a flagrant violation of executive branch responsibilities and authorities. These truly are red lines and [we] simply cannot allow them to be crossed."

She added, "In the United States of America, no one — no one — is above the law, not even the president. Congress must make clear to the president that firing the special counsel or interfering with his investigation by issuing pardons of essential witnesses is unacceptable and would have immediate and significant consequences… [T]here are troubling signs. It is critical that all of us—as elected officials and as citizens — speak up against these threats now before it's too late."

As 2017 moved into 2018...Trump said "no collusion" thousands of times. The Republicans changed from support of Mueller to opposition. People started looking for ways to remove him from his position. According to Politico, Nunes started leading a group of Republicans on the House Intelligence Committee in a secret effort "to build a case that senior leaders of the Justice Department and FBI improperly, and perhaps criminally, mishandled the contents of [the Steele] dossier." The goal was to highlight what some Republicans saw as corruption and conspiracy in the upper ranks of federal law enforcement. The Republicans could ultimately use the results to discredit Mueller's investigation into whether any Trump aides colluded with Russia during the 2016 campaign or even justify his dismissal.

What About Pence's Involvement?

Pence said he was not one of the senior transition officials Flynn reported were aware of his conversations with the Russian ambassador. However, other events do link Pence with Flynn and other questionable people. Pence was chosen Trump's running mate on July 16, 2016. In October, in an interview with Fox News, he said the media were chasing after unsubstantiated allegations that the Trump campaign was working with WikiLeaks. "Nothing could be further from the truth," he emphasized.

When Pence was elected VP, he took over the transition team, with Flynn as Vice Chair. At this time, Obama was already warning Trump against hiring Flynn. Pence received a letter from Representative Cummings of the House Oversight Committee, which questioned Flynn's lobbying work for Russia and Turkey. Cummings asked Pence for the information Flynn had

shared with the transition team as well as a signed letter from Flynn that he did not have any conflict of interest.

When Obama signed an EO on sanctions against Russia for election interference. Kislyak contacted Flynn. In his plea agreement, Flynn said he then called "a senior official of the transition team for guidance on talking with Kislyak." Flynn called Kislyak and asked him not to "escalate the situation," and then reported back to the same senior transition official. *The Washington Post* reported that Flynn spoke several times during this sanctions period. On

"Face the Nation," Pence said "they (Flynn and Kislyak) did not discuss anything having to do with the United States' decision to expel Russian diplomats or ensure Russia. Pence also stated there was not any contact between the transition team and Russia during the campaign. To believe this gave "credence to some of these bizarre rumors that have swirled around the candidacy." *The Washington Post* reported that neither of Pence's comments jived with the complete picture of Flynn's communications with Kislyak as seen in U.S. intelligence monitoring of Russian diplomats.

After the inauguration, Yates told the White House counsel that top officials including Pence made statements about Flynn's actions that were not true. NBC News reported that Pence learned about Yates' warning, and *The Washington Post* said Flynn discussed sanctions with Kislyak. Flynn resigned, noting he had "inadvertently briefed the Vice President-elect and others with incomplete information regarding my phone calls with the Russian ambassador." Pence's spokesperson said the Vice President became aware of incomplete information that he had received from media accounts. He then did an inquiry based on those media accounts. Pence also told Fox News he was just learning about Flynn's work for Turkey through media reports.

A few months later in May, Pence participated in an Oval Office meeting in which Trump reviewed a draft of a letter that summarized reasons for firing Comey. These included the President's unease that Comey would not publicly say Trump was not being investigated.

Comey was fired with the suggestion that it was because of the mishandling of Clinton's email investigation. Pence repeated the explanation that Comey was out because of Rosenstein's recommendation. As noted, Trump had changed that explanation in a TV interview: He was going to fire Comey no matter what.

When Mueller was hired as special counsel, the *New York Times* reported that Trump's team did know Flynn was under investigation for secretly working as a Turkey lobbyist. Pence stood by his earlier claim that he did not know about this..

After the news came out about Donald, Jr.'s meeting with the Russians' promise to get Clinton dirt, Pence's spokesperson said the Vice President was "not aware of the meeting," because it was before he joined the ticket.

Donald, Jr. publicly showed several messages exchanged in 2016 with WikiLeaks. That same day, Pence's spokesperson said the Vice President never knew about anyone working with the campaign being in contact with WikiLeaks.

How much did Pence know about Flynn's Turkey involvement, Donald Jr.'s conversations with Russia, WikiLeaks and Comey's firing has not yet been determined.

Christopher Hayes ✔
@chrislhayes

Stressing this is big: Pence said he'd never heard of the Flynn foreign agent issue, but he was head of transition. Maybe he lied?

CHAPTER TWELVE: FINAL MEANDERINGS

Trump was interviewed by *The New York Time* in December 2017 with repetitious repetition and ongoing meandering during the 30 minutes. He said "no collusion" 16 times. The following is the rough transcript before the final editing in the paper. Some comments have been removed, as have some of the Schmidt's questions. The interview said a great deal about Trump, his mindset and emotional state.

MICHAEL S. SCHMIDT: You're O.K. with me recording, right?

TRUMP: Yeah. Virtually every Democrat has said there is no collusion. There is no collusion. And even these committees that have been set up. If you look at what's going on — and in fact, what it's done is, it's really angered the base and made the base stronger. My base is stronger than it's ever been. Great congressmen, in particular, some of the congressmen have been unbelievable in pointing out what a witch hunt the whole thing is. So, I think it's been proven that there is no collusion.

And by the way, I didn't deal with Russia. I won because I was a better candidate by a lot. I won because I campaigned properly and she didn't. She campaigned for the popular vote. I campaigned for the Electoral College. And you know, it is a totally different thing, Mike. You know the Electoral College, it's like a track star. If you're going to run the 100-yard dash, you work out differently than if you're going to run the 1,000 meters or the mile.

And it's different. It's in golf. If you have a tournament and you have match play or stroke play, you prepare differently, believe it or not. It's different. Match play is very different than stroke play. And you prepare. So I went to Maine five times, I went to [inaudible], the genius of the Electoral College is that you go to places you might not go to.

And that's exactly what [inaudible]. Otherwise, I would have gone to New York, California, Texas and Florida.

SCHMIDT: You would have run completely differently.

TRUMP: It would have been a whole different thing. The genius is that the popular vote is a much different form of campaigning. Hillary never understood that.

SCHMIDT: What's your expectation on Mueller? When do you —

TRUMP: I have no expectation. I can only tell you that there is absolutely no collusion. Everybody knows it. And you know who knows it better than anybody? The Democrats. They walk around blinking at each other.

SCHMIDT: But when do you think he'll be done in regards to you —

TRUMP: I don't know.

SCHMIDT: But does that bother you?

TRUMP: No, it doesn't bother me because I hope that he's going to be fair. I think that he's going to be fair. And based on that [inaudible]. There's been no collusion. But I think he's going to be fair. And if he's fair — because everybody knows the answer already, Michael. I want you to treat me fairly. O.K.?

TRUMP: Maybe I'll just say a little bit of a [inaudible]. I've always found Paul Manafort to be a very nice man. And I found him to be an honorable person. Paul only worked for me for a few months. Paul worked for Ronald Reagan. His firm worked for John McCain, worked for Bob Dole, worked for many Republicans for far longer than he worked for me. And you're talking about what Paul was many years ago before I ever heard of him. He worked for me for — what was it, three and a half months?

 Three and a half months. [Inaudible] So, that's that. Let's just say — I think that Bob Mueller will be fair, and everybody knows that there was no collusion. I saw Dianne Feinstein the other day on television saying there is no collusion. She's the head of the committee. The Republicans, in terms of the House committees, they come out, they're so angry because there is no collusion. So, I actually think that it's turning out — I actually think it's turning to the Democrats because there was collusion on behalf of the Democrats. There was collusion with the Russians and the Democrats. A lot of collusion.

For purposes of the Justice Department, I watched Alan Dershowitz the other day, who by the way, says I, says this is a ridiculous —

SCHMIDT: He's been very good to you.

TRUMP: He's been amazing. And he's a liberal Democrat. I don't know him. He's a liberal Democrat. I watched Alan Dershowitz the other day, he said, No. 1, there is no collusion, No. 2, collusion is not a crime, but even if it was a crime, there was no collusion. And he said that very strongly. He said there was no collusion. And he has studied this thing very closely. I've seen him a number of times. There is no collusion, and even if there was, it's not a crime. But there's no collusion. I don't even say [inaudible]. I don't even go that far.

TRUMP: So for the purposes of what's going on with this phony Russian deal, which, by the way, you've heard me say it, is only an excuse for losing an election that they should have won, because it's very hard for a Republican to win the Electoral College. O.K.? You start off with New York, California and Illinois against you. That means you have to run the East Coast, which I did, and everything else. Which I did and then won Wisconsin and Michigan. [Inaudible.] So the Democrats. … [Inaudible.] … They thought there was no way for a Republican, not me, a Republican, to win the Electoral College. Well, they're [inaudible]. They made the Russian story up as a hoax, as a ruse, as an excuse for losing an election that in theory Democrats should always win with the Electoral College. The Electoral College is so much better suited to the Democrats [inaudible]. But it didn't work out that way. And I will tell you they cannot believe that this became a story.

TRUMP: OK., let's get onto your final question, your other question. Had the Democrats come through. …

SCHMIDT: Tell me about that, yeah.

TRUMP: And if I did bipartisan, I would have done something with SALT [the state and local tax deduction]. With that being said, you look back, Ronald Reagan wanted to take deductibility away from states. Ronald Reagan, years ago, and he couldn't do it. Because New York had a very powerful group of people. Which they don't have today. Today, they don't have the same representatives. You know, in those days they had Lew Rudin and me. … I fought like hell for that. They had a lot of very good guys. Lew Rudin was very effective. He worked hard for New York. And we had some very good senators. … You know, we had a lot of people who fought very hard against, let's call it SALT. Had they come to me and said, look, we'll do this, this, this, we'll do [inaudible]. I could have done something with SALT. Or made it less severe. But they were very ineffective. They were very, very ineffective. You understand what I mean. Had they come to me for a bipartisan tax bill, I would have gone to Mitch, and I would have gone out bipartisan. And that could've been either a change to SALT or knockout of SALT.

But, just so you understand, Ronald Reagan wanted to take deductibility away and he was unable to do it. Ronald Reagan wanted to have ANWR approved 40 years ago and he was unable to do it. Think of that. And the individual mandate is the most unpopular thing in Obamacare, and I got rid of it. You know, we gained with the individual. … You know the individual mandate, Michael, means you take money and you give it to the government for the privilege of not having to pay more money to have health insurance you don't want. There are people who had very good health insurance that now are paying not to have health insurance. That's what the individual mandate. … They're not going to have to pay anymore. So when people think that will be unpopular. … It's going to be very popular. It's going to be very popular.

Now, in my opinion, they should come to me on infrastructure. They should come to me, which they have come to me, on DACA. We are working. … We're trying to something about it. And they should definitely come to me on health care. Because we can do bipartisan health care. We can do bipartisan infrastructure. And we can do bipartisan DACA.

SCHMIDT: What are you willing to do on infrastructure? How far are you willing to go? How much money?

TRUMP: I actually think we can get as many Democrat votes as we have Republican. Republicans want to see infrastructure. Michael, we have spent, as of about a month ago, $7 trillion in the Middle East. And the Middle East is worse than it was 17 years ago. … [Inaudible.] $7 trillion. And if you want $12 to fix up a road or a highway, you can't get it. I want to do a trillion-dollar infrastructure bill, at least. We want to fix our roads, our highways, our bridges, which are in bad shape. And you know some of them are actually, they're x-ed out, they have, you know, possibilities of collapse under bad circumstances. And in 10 years they will collapse. So, I want a trillion-dollar infrastructure plan. I think it can be bipartisan. I believe we can do health care in a bipartisan way, because now we've essentially gutted and ended Obamacare.

TRUMP: So now I have associations, I have private insurance companies coming and will sell private health care plans to people through associations. That's gonna be millions and millions of people. People have no idea how big that is. And by the way, and for that, we've ended across state lines. So we have competition. You know for that I'm allowed to [inaudible] state lines. So that's all done.

Now I've ended the individual mandate. And the other thing I wish you'd tell people. So when I do this, and we've got healthcare, you know, McCain did his vote. … But what we have. I had a hundred congressmen that said no and I was able to talk them into it. They're great people.

Two things: No. 1, I have unbelievably great relationships with 97 percent of the Republican congressmen and senators. I love them and they love me. That's No. 1. And No. 2, I know more about the big bills. … [Inaudible.] … Than any president that's ever been in office. Whether it's health care and taxes. Especially taxes. And if I didn't, I couldn't have persuaded a hundred. … You ask Mark Meadows [inaudible]. … I couldn't have persuaded a hundred congressmen to go along with the bill. The first bill, you know, that was ultimately, shockingly rejected.

So, the taxes. … [Inaudible.] … The tax cut will be, the tax bill, prediction, will be far bigger than anyone imagines. Expensing will be perhaps the greatest of all provisions. Where you can do something, you can buy something. … Piece of equipment. … You can do lots of different things, and you can write it off and expense it in one year. That will be one of the great stimuli in history. You watch. That'll be one of the big. … People don't even talk about expensing, what's the word "expensing." [Inaudible.] One year expensing. Watch the money coming back into the country, it'll be more money than people anticipate.

But Michael, I know the details of taxes better than anybody. Better than the greatest C.P.A. I know the details of health care better than most, better than most. And if I didn't, I couldn't have talked all these people into doing ultimately only to be rejected.

Now here's the good news. We've created associations, millions of people are joining associations. Millions. That were formerly in Obamacare or didn't have insurance. Or didn't have health care. Millions of people. That's gonna be a big bill, you watch. It could be as high as 50 percent of the people. You watch. So that's a big thing. And the individual mandate. So now you have associations, and people don't even talk about the associations. That could be half the people are going to be joining up. … With private [inaudible]. So now you have associations and the individual mandate.

I believe that because of the individual mandate and the associations, the Democrats will and certainly should come to me and see if they can do a really great health care plan for the remaining people. [Inaudible.]

SCHMIDT: And you think you can do it?

TRUMP: Well, we're perfectly set up to do it. See, it was hard for them to do it as long as the individual mandate existed. But now that the individual mandate is officially killed, people have no idea how big a deal that was. It's the most unpopular part of Obamacare. But now, Obamacare is essentially. … You know, you saw this. … It's basically dead over a period of time.

SCHMIDT: Yeah.

TRUMP: But the Democrats should come to a bipartisan bill. And we can fix it. We can fix it. We can make a great health care plan. Not Obamacare, which was a bad plan. We can make a great health care plan through bipartisanship. We can do a great infrastructure plan through bipartisanship. And we can do on immigration, and DACA in particular, we can do something that's terrific through bipartisanship.

SCHMIDT: It sounds like you're tacking to the center in a way you didn't before.

TRUMP: No, I'm not being centered. I'm just being practical. No, I don't think I'm changing. Look, I wouldn't do a DACA plan without a wall. Because we need it. We see the drugs pouring into the country, we need the wall.

SCHMIDT: So you're not moving. You're saying I'm more likely to do deals, but I'm not moving.

TRUMP: I'm always moving, moving in both directions. We have to get rid of chainlike immigration, we have to get rid of the chain. The chain is the last guy that killed. … [Talking with guests.] … The last guy that killed the eight people. … [Inaudible.] … So badly wounded people. … Twenty-two people came in through chain migration. Chain migration and the lottery system. They have a lottery in these countries.

They take the worst people in the country, they put 'em into the lottery, then they have a handful of bad, worse ones, and they put them out. 'Oh, these are the people the United States. …" … We're gonna get rid of the lottery, and by the way, the Democrats agree with me on that. On chain migration, they pretty much agree with me.

SCHMIDT: Do you think I'm wrong to think next year could be the year of you being a real deal maker, in a way you maybe weren't in the past year?

TRUMP: I was. I make deals with the Republicans. I had nobody to make a deal with the Democrats. The Democrats could have made a much better tax deal for Democrats if they came to see us, but they didn't come. They never thought I'd be able to get this over the line. And especially when McCain, when John McCain left and went to Arizona, they thought they had it made.

SCHMIDT: What's going on there (China). Tell me about that.

TRUMP: Yeah, China. ... China's been. ... I like very much President Xi. He treated me better than anybody's ever been treated in the history of China. You know that. The presentations. ... One of the great two days of anybody's life and memory having to do with China. He's a friend of mine, he likes me, I like him, we have a great chemistry together. He's [inaudible] of the United States. ...[Inaudible.] China's hurting us very badly on trade, but I have been soft on China because the only thing more important to me than trade is war. O.K.?

I can tell you one thing: This is a problem that should have been handled for the last 25 years. This is a problem, North Korea. That should have been handled for 25, 30 years, not by me. This should have been handled long before me. Long before this guy has whatever he has.

TRUMP: No, look, I like China, and I like him a lot. But, as you know, when I campaigned, I was very tough on China in terms of trade. They made — last year, we had a trade deficit with China of $350 billion, minimum. That doesn't include the theft of intellectual property, O.K., which is another $300 billion. So, China — and you know, somebody said, oh, currency manipulation. If they're helping me with North Korea, I can look at trade a little bit differently, at least for a period of time. And that's what I've been doing. But when oil is going in, I'm not happy about that. I think I expressed that in probably [inaudible].

TRUMP, as aides walk by: And, by the way, it's not a tweet. It's social media, and it gets out in the world, and the reason I do well is that I can be treated unfairly and very dishonestly by CNN, and, you know, I have — what do have now, John, 158 million, including Facebook, including Twitter, including Instagram, including every form, I have a 158 million people. Reporting just this morning, they said 158 million. So if they a do a story that's false, I can do something — otherwise, Andy, otherwise you just sort of walk around saying what can I do? What, am I going to have a press conference every time somebody, every time Michael writes something wrong?

So, China on trade has ripped off this country more than any other element of the world in history has ripped off anything. But I can be different if they're helping us with North Korea. If they don't help us with North Korea, then I do what I've always said I want to do. China can help us much more, and they have to help us much more. And they have to help us much more. We have a nuclear menace out there, which is no good for China, and it's not good for Russia. It's no good for anybody. Does that make sense?

SCHMIDT: Yeah, yeah, it makes a lot of sense.

Conclusion: Good News!

Women's March. According to data compiled by Erica Chenoweth at the University of Denver and Jeremy Pressman at the University of Connecticut, at least 3.3 million people participated in over 500 marches across the country. Estimates show one out of every 100 Americans participated in the march. The Women's March in Washington was three times bigger, or more, than the crowd at Trump's inauguration. Plus, women marched on all seven continents across the world.

Protests against Trump. People around the U.S. and the world protested from the first day Trump was elected against him and their government representatives. These protests were about specific legislation and government direction, as well as to the President's rhetoric.. Some protests have taken the form of walk-outs, business closures, petitions, rallies, demonstrations or marches. While most protests have been peaceful, some destroyed property and caused physical harm to others. Protestors met in the streets, at public events, at the Congresspeople's offices and to Congress, itself.

Me-Too in 2018. Through the Women's March and the "Me-Too" Movement that publicized the men who harassed and abused women, increasing numbers of women decided to run for office in 2018. 2018 will see a record number of female congressional candidates. By March of 2018, over 430 women said they planned on running for the House. The number of female Senate candidates is expected to double from 25 to 50. Most of the women are Democratic because of the Trump backlash, but the GOP will also have new contenders for Congress and governor races. .

The verdict is out on the status of Trump next year at this time. Whether or not I write book *Second Year of Hell* is anyone's guess. History has shown that change moves slowly in Washington when a private counsel is investigating an issue or a specific person. Even when recommendations are made to initiate impeachment proceedings or prosecute individuals, Congress does not have to follow through. Richard Nixon resigned his Presidency and he was not impeached by the House of Representatives. Nor does impeachment proceedings necessarily mean that the President will be found guilty. Nixon is one of three U.S. Presidents against whom articles of impeachment were reported to the full House for consideration. The other two–Andrew Johnson in 1868 and Bill Clinton in 1998–were impeached and acquitted ; from all charges following a Senate trial.

Both Johnson and Clinton were impeached in the House on two counts, but not removed by the Senate. President Nixon resigned before the impeachment was completed in the House, since he knew the Senate would have voted to remove him.

Trump Administration may be a threat to U.S. democracy, but the President and his cabinet and advisors are only part of the problem. Most Republicans have spent the past year doing their best to shield Trump from being investigated. With Senators such as Nunes, this shielding has bordered on the absurd, with either made up or edited information being used to defend Trump and slam the Democrats. Even Ryan and McConnell have ignored flagrant violations.

In March of 2018, the Republican House Intelligence Committee ended their investigation, despite many relevant people not being interviewed or, if they were, pleading exemptions instead of responding to questions. The committee concluded that there "was no collusion" between anyone from the Trump campaign and Russia. The Democrats refused to accept this conclusion and, in fact, issued a rebuttal. "The work is too important to be left undone," Representative Adam Schiff said. "The American people need to know whether the Russians still have something they can hold over the President's head." Schiff called the GOP report "little more than another Nunes memo in long form." Regardless of distinct differences of opinion about collusion, Schiff and others hoped Democrats and Republicans could jointly validate the conclusion of intelligence agencies that Russia sought to elect Trump. "If this is where the GOP is coming from, it represents to me the completeness of their capitulation to the White House, and that leaves little common ground," Schiff said.

As this book goes to press, the country is nearing the 2018 Congressional election, with some special elections before this. Right now, it appears that the Democrats will have a major impact on these elections. The world may perhaps look more hopeful a year from now.

AFTER READING MY BOOK, PLEASE TAKE A FEW MINUTES TO SUBMIT A REVIEW. ALSO, SHARE THE BOOK WITH OTHERS OR GIVE THEM THEIR OWN COPY. THE MORE INFORMATION WE HAVE, THE MORE WE CAN FIGHT AGAINST ANY THREATS TO DEMOCRATIC IDEALS.

Thank You!!!
Sharon

www.ingramcontent.com/pod-product-compliance
Lightning Source LLC
Chambersburg PA
CBHW081839250726
48659CB00008B/2517